Praise for *Green Nails and Other Acts of Rebellion*

"Elaine Soloway's essays on caregiving and widowhood are important reading. They not only engage and stimulate, but also help senior women face new challenges, and share a sense of dignity and celebration."

—Tam Gray,
SeniorWomen.com

"Soloway wins the day with her upbeat essays, showing us that there is 'life after loss' as she soldiers on in her seventies, to more joy and happiness, embracing a life filled with love and laughter from friends and family."

—Sandy Pesman,
WidowsList.com

"Soloway's story delves deeper than the role of caregiver to her husband. It's not so much about Tommy as it is about coping with his illness and learning to live with it. It's about accepting life's challenges and moving forward, even when forward sometimes feels backward. It's a story that manages to stay surprisingly lighthearted, as Soloway injects bittersweet memories and bits of humor into her writing. There is no woe-is-me moment in this book. There is no asking of sympathy. I always respect that in a writer."

—Sophie L. Nagelberg,
LiteraryChicago.com

GREEN NAILS
AND
OTHER ACTS
OF
REBELLION

GREEN NAILS
AND
OTHER ACTS
OF
REBELLION

Life After Loss

Elaine Soloway

SHE WRITES PRESS

Published 2014
Printed in the United States of America
ISBN: 978-1-63152-919-1
Library of Congress Control Number: 2014939004

For information, address:
She Writes Press
1563 Solano Ave #546
Berkeley, CA 94707

There are as many versions of every family's history as there are family members. This is mine. Some names of people and places have been changed.

In memory of my husband, Thomas Madison
August 24, 1935–November 2, 2012

Contents

Now May I Shoot the Messenger?...............1

Tommy Sleeps Through the Night 4

Matching Bands............................6

Strongman 9

The Wrong War...........................11

Sunday Breakfast.........................14

Paint by Number.........................17

The Artist Prefers to Work Alone 20

Easy Rider...............................23

Unpacking 25

Four Times Around 28

Food and Music—A Perfect Match............31

Learning to Un-drive 34

Grateful He's a Tightwad 37

Take Care of Yourself 40

Do You Have a Visual? 43

Green Thumb............................46

The Screening Room.......................49

Toolshed 52

All for One, One for All 55

Softy. 58

Crime Scene Investigation: Chicago 60

When the Caregiver Needs Care 63

The Turnaround Tango. 66

The Kids Are All Right 68

Better Late Than Never. 71

Tommy Untucked 74

Prince Charming. 77

How to Suction a Tracheotomy. 80

An Untroubled Brow. 82

The Ambivalent Widow 85

Sunday Breakfast, Minus One 87

Ma's Home 90

The Takeover 92

The Opposite of Caregiving. 95

The Handyman 98

Like Mother, Like Daughter. Or Not 101

Odd Number 104

Growing Stronger 107

Without a Trace. 110

The Sign 113

Un-couching the Potato 116

Carless in Chicago. 119

Chatterbox 122

Painting Furniture 124

Roommate 127

Rolling the Dice. 130

A Dollhouse, Part Two 133

My Psyche and Its Five Stages 136

Coed Majoring in Phys Ed 139

Re-couching the Potato .142

The Men in My Life 145

Green Nails and Other Acts of Rebellion 148

Fights of Fancy 151

Empty-Nest Syndrome, Part Two 154

Head Trip 157

Body Type 160

Swell Party 163

Homeward Bound 166

California Dreaming 169

Forget Him Not 172

I'll Call You 175

Déjà vu 178

Jealousy at the Gym 181

From Third Wheel to Driver's Seat 184

A Resting Place in the Garden of Eden 187

Double-Dating with My Mother 190

Offended 2013 193

Ink Fades, but Memories Linger 196

To Be Adored 199

Acknowledgments 202

Questions for Discussion 204

Resources 206

About the Author 208

One:
Now, May I Shoot the Messenger?

Early in 2009, I wanted to write a novel. The plot was outlined in my head: a woman, unhappy in her marriage, would abandon her husband and run away to New York.

At the time, my imaginary plot mirrored my life. I fantasized about leaving a note for Tommy, telling him I'd get in touch when I was settled. I didn't think he would care.

I never did write the novel, nor run away. Instead, I made an appointment with my therapist.

"My husband is a jerk," I told Sarah. "When we first married, he'd write me love letters, hide Post-it notes with 'Love you, Wifey' in my gym bag. Now, nothing."

Sarah sat across from me in her small office. I sank into the cushions of her couch, and into my own self-pity, as I had done at other sad or puzzling times in my life.

"He doesn't care about me," I whined. "He never asks about my day. I'll say, 'How was the Y? How was golf?' But me? It's like I don't exist."

I continued, "And he bursts out with these stupid comments. He shouts at the television set. 'You're an actor,' he'll say to a commercial. 'You're fat!' he throws at Oprah. I've tried to reason with him, but it's no use; he just repeats the same dumb thing the next time a housewife selling soap or Oprah appears on the screen."

Sarah listened. She didn't nod, pitying my plight. She didn't agree my husband was a jerk. She didn't encourage my escape. "Do you want to live alone?" she asked.

I pictured Tommy on his own. He'd probably survive. Before

we married, in 1998, he'd been a bachelor for fifteen years. He knew how to cook, clean, take care of himself. But I couldn't stand being alone. After my first husband walked out of our thirty-year marriage, all I wanted was to be part of a couple again.

Sarah's questioned lingered. I thought about the early years of my marriage to Tommy. Our compatibility, our comfortable evenings at home—my husband on the couch, working on the crossword puzzle; me opposite, reading a newspaper. We were happy together.

"No," I told Sarah, as I reached for the box of Kleenex. "I don't want to live alone."

As my sessions with Sarah continued, something was happening with Tommy. He was having trouble speaking. I asked him if he saw the words in his head. He nodded. "But you can't get them out of your mouth?" Another yes. He could start the crossword puzzle but could not finish it. Some people thought his garbled language meant he was drunk.

"Perhaps he should see a neurologist," Sarah said when I described his latest behavior.

His internist agreed. Over several months late in 2009, Tommy had blood tests, an EEG, a neuropsychometric test, and a brain SPECT scan.

"Don't shoot the messenger" was how the neurologist put it. He turned to me, as if Tommy were already unable to understand what was coming. "I suspect your husband has primary progressive aphasia. It's a dementia that affects the frontal lobe, the brain's language center. There is no cure, and the experimental drugs can cause hallucinations or other side effects."

He went on talking, about follow-up visits for Tommy, a support group for me. We rose from our chairs and left the office hand in hand. As we walked to the subway, I turned to Tommy and asked, "Are you okay?"

"I don't have dementia," he said.

"I know, honey, I know," I said, squeezing his hand.

As soon as we arrived home, I looked up the symptoms associated with the illness. They matched every complaint I had unleashed in Sarah's office, plus some I had never gotten around to disclosing. I learned it typically started early, often in one's sixties, and was slow moving. Tommy must have had it for years before the speech problems surfaced.

Once I knew the diagnosis and symptoms, my anger toward my husband evaporated. I no longer wanted to write the novel or run away. I ended therapy. I understood my husband was not responsible for his behavior. He could do nothing to stop his actions. I became empathetic and compassionate.

In 2012 three years after the diagnosis, Tommy can barely speak. Primary progressive aphasia has completed its task. Post-it notes once holding sentiments of love are now used for clues when I get stumped. I value these written words as much as I did the love notes.

Our marriage is happy and as companionable as his illness allows. Today, when we watch television together, on couches that face each other, my husband no longer yells at the commercials, or at Oprah.

Two:
Tommy Sleeps Through the Night

I'm on the living room couch, watching the numbers on the DVR's digital clock. It's three thirty in the morning, and I'm praying Tommy doesn't wake up before his alarm, like he did yesterday.

It was 3:45 a.m. when he hustled out of bed and started pulling on his jeans.

"Honey, it's three forty-five in the morning," I told my husband. I pulled his elbow and tried to stop him from putting his belt through the loop.

Tommy pulled away and moved to lace his tennis shoes. He didn't rebut because he can't speak. With his condition of PPA progressing quickly, we're left with bits of common language from our fourteen-year marriage. And, if we're lucky, a written note.

At least he's safe in bed, I tell myself.

At least he's no longer driving.

It was my neighbor across the street who called to tell me Tommy had sideswiped another car and driven off. I was waiting for this kind of call, for I worried every time he got in his car. If he was late coming home from the Y or from his golf date, I'd pace in front of the window until I saw his Honda Accord pull into the driveway.

"You have to take away the keys before he kills someone," my daughter said when I told her of the latest incident. "You'll never forgive yourself."

So, neighbors Holly and John sat on the couch with me to tell Tommy it was no longer safe for him to drive. When he refused to give me his car keys, I said, "John will remove the battery." I got that line from one of his neurologists.

"We've got lots of kids in the neighborhood," Holly said. "You can't be driving."

"No," Tommy said. "Golf, the Y." He could get those words out.

"I'll take you," I said. "Anywhere you want to go."

Yesterday when Tommy woke at 3:45 a.m., I followed him downstairs to the living room. He settled on the couch and turned on the remote. He wrote on a Post-it, "Rock."

Aha! Tommy thought he had been taking his afternoon nap and it was time to get up and watch one of his favorite TV shows, *The Rockford Files*. When I opened the curtains to show him it was still dark outside, when I went through the MeTV listings to show him there was no Rockford, when I pointed to the "a.m." on the TV screen's time, he clicked the remote and went back upstairs to bed.

This morning, it appears he is sleeping through.

Three:
Matching Bands

In 1998, when Tommy and I got married, we went to Service Merchandise to buy matching gold wedding bands. It was the second marriage for both of us; we were in our sixties. I think we paid $25 for each. Fancy gems weren't important to us back then—still aren't.

This year, 2012, our gold rings still encircle our fingers, but we've added an accessory just a few inches below these symbols of our union.

We wear matching black flex bands with two-inch-wide stainless-metal plates. Engraving on the front side of Tommy's reads TOM MADISON, APHASIA, CHICAGO. On the inside it says CALL WIFE, ELAINE SOLOWAY and my cell phone number.

While Tommy's band is size 7, mine is 6. Engraved on the front side of mine is simply ELAINE SOLOWAY, CHICAGO. Thus far, I have no medical issue that requires explanation. Arthritis doesn't count, does it?

On the reverse of my band: IN EMERGENCY, H. SOLOWAY, MD, with my ex-husband's cell phone number. The two bands cost $46.90, including shipping and handling, nearly the same as our gold ones.

I ordered our medical alert bracelets after Tommy got lost. "You shouldn't let him travel alone," one of my daughters had warned. But I knew he treasured his CTA senior card, and I believed since all previous trips had returned him home safely, he'd be fine. I had already taken away his car keys. I hated the idea of robbing him of one more symbol of independence.

On the afternoon Tommy got lost, he was on his way to see his speech therapist. Her office is at Michigan Avenue between Randolph and Washington in Chicago. One hour and fifteen minutes after he left, the home phone rang. No one except marketers called on this line, and I'd urged Tommy to use only my cell. But I answered it.

Dead air. Finally, garbled words.

"Honey, where are you?" I said. I held on to my desk.

"Mmmm," he got out.

"Are you in the subway?" I envisioned him in the depths, alone, scared. My grip tightened.

"Mmmm," he repeated.

"Tommy," I pleaded, "please find someone you can hand the phone to."

I was grateful he carried his cell phone, grateful he could punch in the number—even if it was the landline—but terrified about how to find him.

Finally, a female voice. "Hi, this is Marcello's."

"Marcello's on North Ave. and Halsted?" I asked.

"Yes."

"Tell my husband to wait there. I'm on my way."

"Oh, he's okay," she said. "He just bought a slice of coffee cake."

You know those photos of people doing superhuman feats in an emergency? Wee women lifting automobiles off of trapped victims?

It was 4:30 p.m., rush hour in Chicago, and I was about to drive five miles from our house to the intersection of North Avenue, Halsted Street, and Clybourn Avenue—the traffic triangle from hell. But I was superhuman.

I put the leash on the dog and got in the car, and together we slogged along I-90 to North Avenue and then crept east to the restaurant. At every mile, I thanked God, grateful Tommy was found, grateful he was okay, grateful he ate coffee cake.

My husband was seated on a bench outside the restaurant. "How did you get here?" I asked. Before getting into the passenger seat, Tommy opened the back door and patted Buddy's head.

The best I can figure from Tommy's "yes" and "no" responses is that he exited the subway at Washington and Dearborn, as usual. Then he got confused and started walking. And he walked the three miles to Marcello's.

When the medical alert bands arrived a few days after this episode, I thought Tommy would balk at putting his on because he doesn't like to cop to his illness. But this time, no argument; he slipped it on.

My own medical alert band, with my ex's information, was necessary because I can no longer list Tommy as an emergency contact. "Do you mind?" I asked my ex. We were married for thirty years, he knows my doctors and has our daughters' phone numbers plugged into his cell, and I knew the "MD" after his name meant I'd get immediate attention. And we are blessed with a good relationship.

"No problem," he said.

I wear my medical alert band only when I leave the house. But the gold ring hasn't left my finger—or Tommy's—since the ecumenical minister who married us in Las Vegas encouraged their mutual exchange.

In that ceremony, as we slipped gold bands on each other's finger, we echoed the clergyman's words. "In sickness and in health," we vowed.

Four:
Strongman

Tommy can bench-press his own weight. He's been a member of the Lakeview YMCA for forty years—showing up every Monday, Wednesday, and Friday. At first, he was in the 6:00 p.m. crowd, then, after retiring, the 9:00 a.m. one. I credit my seventy-six-year-old husband's great physical shape to this dedication.

On one recent morning, I was leading the way through the kitchen to the garage to drive Tommy to the Y. He was following behind, zipping his coat, donning his knit cap with the Bears logo, and hoisting a gym bag onto his shoulder. As I passed the counter where he stows his eyeglasses and cell phone, I noticed something was missing.

"Tommy," I said, turning to catch my husband's attention, "where's the medical ID band I bought for you?"

I wanted him to wear the band everywhere, including the Y. Although he has been a regular for many years, there's no guarantee he'd be known. Employees leave, members drop out, and his speech problems make it unlikely he's met new people. My worst scenario: Tommy injured, unable to say his name or mine. A crowd coming to his rescue. "I think his name is Bill," someone says. "But I have no idea of his last name."

Now the band with his name, his diagnosis, and my phone number was missing. I didn't see it on his wrist. It was not on the counter where his other accessories awaited him.

"Where's the band?" I asked again.

Tommy pointed to the front hallway. I reversed directions and headed for the straw basket that sits under the table. That's where we toss advertising flyers and unwanted mail.

"Did you throw it out?" I asked.

Another "no." He opened one of the table's drawers and pointed to the medical ID band stuffed inside.

"You have to wear this," I said, and retrieved the band from where it mingled with extra keys, a rack-like tool we use to groom the dog, tubes of ChapStick, abandoned sunglasses, and other detritus.

I handed the band to Tommy, and we continued our exit to the door. Once we were seated in the car, I turned to him in the passenger seat. "Is it uncomfortable?" I asked. "Is that why you don't want to wear it?" He nodded "yes."

"Well, wear it only when you leave the house," I said.

The next morning, Tommy's reading glasses and cell phone were in their usual place, but no medical ID band. He hadn't worn it to bed. It wasn't on his bedside table or in the bathroom. I searched the hallway table drawer. I searched the kitchen. I found the band on the counter, hidden behind a giant-size jar of dog vitamins.

I didn't ask Tommy why he refuses to wear the band to the Y. I think I've figured it out. The gym is his sanctuary, free of a hovering wife. It is the place where he doesn't have to talk; where he is proud of his three-times-a-week attendance and his routine of thirty-three minutes on the elliptical, then twenty minutes of weight lifting. At the Y, he is a strongman, not someone needing a medical ID bracelet.

Later that day, I called the executive director of the Y. I told her Tommy's diagnosis. I gave her my cell phone number. "Thank you so much," she said. "I'll put the information in Tom's file and make sure the staff knows who he is, and his condition. I really appreciate your sharing this."

Tommy is strong; I'm shaping up.

Five:
The Wrong War

In 1956, when he was twenty-one, Tommy enlisted in the US Air Force, where he trained as a radio operator. Eventually, he rose to the rank of corporal and was stationed in Japan until he was honorably discharged in 1959.

I didn't know Tommy in his youth; we didn't meet until 1996, and then married two years later. But I often pictured that affable boy in those long-ago days—trim in his uniform, cap atop his military crew cut, proud to serve his country.

Those images surfaced recently when I dug through my husband's papers to learn if he would be eligible for a US Department of Veterans Affairs benefit called Aid and Attendance.

If he passed the test, the VA would pay up to $1,644 per month to hire a home health aide. The application for benefits required a copy of Tommy's separation papers, a medical evaluation from a physician, and a list of current medical issues. The Air Force papers were in my hand. His diagnosis of primary progress aphasia was filed in the folder marked BRAIN.

For nearly a year, my daughters—who live in Los Angeles and Boston—had been urging me to find someone who could stay overnight with Tommy. They were disappointed that I halted my travels after I believed it was no longer safe to leave my husband home alone. I knew he could handle normal activities, but what if he had to call for help? His aphasia would render him powerless in any emergency calls to 911 or neighbors.

When he was well, I traveled to either coast at least three times a year. Tommy, a stepfather who became bored by my desire to do nothing but stare at my grandchildren or shadow my daughters, opted to stay put at home and take care of the dog.

While away, I would call him nightly. "Get your butt home," he'd tease. Then, I knew all was fine. But eventually, that phrase was absent. Or if he did manage a few words, they were dangerously frayed.

So I saw that $1,644 monthly benefit as my salvation. That would be enough money to enlist the services of a home health agency to give me an occasional break and to be assured Tommy would be tucked safely in his own home if I traveled to fawn over my offspring and theirs.

I studied the amount—one thousand, six hundred, forty-four. I imagined the check directly deposited into my bank account each month. I saw myself handing a set of house keys to a trusted aide who would bid me good-bye with, "Don't worry about a thing. He'll be fine."

Then I looked at this eligibility caveat: "Any war veteran with ninety days of active duty, one day beginning or ending during a period of war."

Period of war? Quickly, I searched for the descriptions. Here's what I found about recent conflicts:

World War II. December 7, 1941, through December 31, 1946, inclusive. If the veteran was in service on December 31, 1946, continuous service before July 26, 1947, is considered World War II service.

Korean conflict. June 27, 1950, through January 31, 1955, inclusive.

Vietnam era. The period beginning on February 28, 1961, and ending on May 7, 1975, inclusive, in the case of a veteran who served in the Republic of Vietnam during that period. The period beginning on August 5, 1964, and ending on May 7, 1975, inclusive, in all other cases.

Do you see 1956–59 in that list? Neither do I. My boyish Tommy, trim in his Air Force uniform, earnestly communicating with his static-filled radio, gung-ho in his military exercises, had served in the wrong war. There would be no $1,644 check slipping monthly into my bank account, no packing of suitcases for the coasts.

Okay, so the VA won't come to my rescue, but no retreat for this caregiving spouse. I'll gather ammunition, devise a battle plan, and tramp ahead. Surrender isn't an option.

Six:
Sunday Breakfast

Our booth at Dapper's is all set with napkins and silverware, ketchup and hot sauce, and miniature capsules of flavored creams that my husband likes in his morning coffee. Linda, our favorite waitress, has taken care of this.

As we approach the setting, Tommy gives my shoulder a squeeze. It is a love tap, I know. We remove our jackets and caps and toss them in a corner of our benches. I extract Tommy's reading glasses from my tote bag while he parcels out the Sunday paper. Once we are settled, Linda approaches with her order pad and pencil.

Every Sunday morning since we first met, Tommy and I have eaten breakfasts out. We are creatures of habit. We like predictability. We are not the sort who seek out the latest place. Routine makes us comfortable, like a pair of favored slippers.

The Lakeview Restaurant, on Ashland Avenue in Chicago, was the first diner we went to as a couple. Tommy, who had lived in the neighborhood for at least twenty years, was a regular. Before I entered the picture, he would sit alone at the counter, reading a paperback, until one of his cronies took the stool next to him.

When Tommy first brought me to the Lakeview, he held my hand as he introduced me to his waitress. "This is Elaine," he said, loudly enough for the other customers to hear. He tightened his grip on my hand, as if he feared I would get away.

Two years later, he held both our hands aloft to show our wedding rings. "My wife," he said. The other diners turned their heads to learn the source of the jubilant voice.

I can't remember the name of our Lakeview waitress, but Tommy likely could. Although he has PPA, the disease has left his memory intact.

Soon after we married, something stirred me to shake predictability and prove I could surprise. After living in the city all my life, I convinced Tommy we should move to a small town. Although my husband was content where we lived in Chicago, he wanted to keep his dopey-dreaming wife happy. So he helped pack.

We found the Geneva Diner in the small town, forty miles west of Chicago. Every Sunday morning, we'd settle into our regular booth and chat up the college student who was our waitress. But the regularity of Sunday breakfast in this bucolic spot—where there were only a handful of Jews (like me) and even fewer Democrats (like both of us)—couldn't make up for my feeling I had made a giant mistake. Exactly one year later, I dragged Tommy back to Chicago.

Once again, my husband, who had planted a vegetable garden and said he could have remained in Geneva, went along with the move. Perhaps he believed that the vow we took in 1998, "Till death do us part," meant following his wife's foolish whims.

We settled in the Independence Park neighborhood on the city's northwest side. I felt free of the itch for a change of scenery. I was finished with surprises. All I wanted was the familiar, the lovely predictability of everyday life.

"Do you want to see a menu, or do you know what you want?" Linda at Dapper asks. She knows we don't want to see a menu but never fails to give us the option. She looks to Tommy, pencil poised. She has been a witness to my husband's steady loss of language over the past three years but has never given a clue there is a problem.

She waits as Tommy voices something that resembles the first syllable of a breakfast dish. Dear Linda catches his choice. She doesn't turn to me, as some people do, to decipher what Tommy is trying to say—and I'll tell you, I don't like it when they do that. She just says, "Got it."

When Linda leaves the table, Tommy passes my favorite newspaper sections to me. He taps my hand. I take this to mean he is happy to be engaged in this predictable, ordinary Sunday ritual. Then we begin flipping pages and reading. With our lack of conversation, we appear to be an old married couple who disdain chatting in favor of the print before us.

Seven:
Paint by Number

I wasn't jealous when Tommy beamed as he led Julie on a tour of our house. He was showing off his paintings and smiled at her, like a teen smitten with a cheerleader.

But later that morning, when my husband revealed something to this art therapist he had not shared with me, I felt as envious as a plain Jane watching from the sidelines.

I had hired Julie to work with Tommy upon the recommendation of the social worker at Northwestern University Feinberg School of Medicine who has been guiding me since my husband's diagnosis.

Julie had prematurely gray hair, was dressed in a black outfit accessorized with colorful scarves, and looked the part of Artist. In some ways, she resembled a younger version of me. I'd like to think that led to Tommy's easy acceptance of her into his therapeutic life.

He had fifteen paint-by-number pictures to show her. They are on walls throughout our house. All are beautiful and match the example on the cover of each kit. Over the years, as Tommy completed each painting, he'd select a frame, tuck the painting into protective glass, then hang it where it could be seen and admired.

Tommy chose paint by number as a winter hobby, when the weather prohibited his favorite pastime, golf. I was happy to see him engaged in something creative. To show my support, I bought an easel for the spare bedroom, a gooseneck lamp to clip to the top of the board, and a French beret to complete the picture of artist's atelier.

For several years, Tommy finished two paintings per season. Then, early in 2012, trouble. His work no longer matched the box's cover. He halted this effort midway, eventually tossing it in the trash. I guessed the cruel illness that was stealing his speech was now affecting his brushstrokes.

So, when Tommy wanted to try again, I was surprised. I helped him choose a new kit from our usual online store and watched as he assembled the easel, attached the light, spread the baby pots of paint on a makeshift table, and started in. (The beret is long gone.) But, after a few days, he stopped. He turned off the lamp, put the brush down alongside the pots, and left the unfinished painting on the easel. Then he closed the door to his studio.

"These are marvelous," Julie said, as Tommy led her through the first floor and pointed to each one of his paintings. When the two of them went upstairs, I could hear her praising the works in the hall and in our bedroom. Then I heard him open the door to the room where the abandoned painting still stood on the easel. I remained downstairs, wondering how artist and teacher would handle what they found.

Julie came down first, with Tommy trailing after her. "We're dumping this," she said, holding the painting in two fingers. My husband was nodding in agreement and grinning. "We're going to start fresh with a new painting." Then she showed me what Tommy had written on a Post-it note. "MESS," it read.

Julie smiled at him as if he were already her favorite student. "Yes," she said, "that's what Tommy was trying to tell me upstairs. That's why we agreed to start a new one."

Mess? My husband had confessed to this stranger how he felt about his abandoned painting? I was jealous; the emotion absent from their first interaction now struck.

I wanted in. "Maybe it would be better to try something free-form," I said. "It might be easier than paint by number."

"No," Julie said, looking to my husband for confirmation. "Tom likes paint by number, so we're going to stick with that."

Then she asked, "Tom, is the problem that the numbered

places are too small or that your brain is having a hard time getting the message to your hand?"

He shook his head at the former and nodded "yes" to the latter.

"Okay," Julie said. "Now we know how to proceed."

After Julie left, I thought about how she was able to get my husband to open up. Perhaps it was her training, her distance from the role of spousal caregiver, and her compassion that gave her the key.

Or, maybe it was because Julie didn't know our backstory: that before the illness, when Tommy could talk, he was a man of a few words, never eager to discuss emotional issues. When I saw the closed door, I assumed Tommy preferred to drop the subject. And perhaps I was relieved I didn't have to enter this emotional territory.

That afternoon, I turned on the computer. Tommy pulled up a chair next to me. We searched the paint-by-number website. He selected *The Ice Cardinal*. It would arrive within three days, in time for our next art therapy.

Eight:
The Artist Prefers to Work Alone

"What about here?" I am holding Tommy's latest paint by number in my hands and stretching to reach a spot on the kitchen wall above the TV.

My husband raises two thumbs up, his catchall for "yes," "okay," "great," and "perfect." We agree *The Ice Cardinal*—a painting of a red bird, white and blue tree limbs, framed in black metal—will look great in this spot.

From a distance, the painting looks colorful, novel. Close inspection reveals this effort—Tommy's latest—does not match the perfection of the fifteen other paint-by-number works he has completed over the years.

No matter. I'm impressed with *The Ice Cardinal* anyway. I had thought his paint-by-number days were over because PPA has erased most of his speech and chipped away at his concentration. Once an avid reader of Ruth Rendell mysteries, Tommy left the last book untouched on the coffee table. Crossword puzzles no longer are attempted. And an older paint by number had stood unfinished on its easel.

On the morning of the second session, I opened the door to the art therapist. My husband lay prone on his couch, as if he were a corpse. She took a seat on the couch opposite him, pulled out a notebook, and began to ask questions that would lead to a plan for ongoing sessions. Looking at Tommy's body language, I suspected she, and I, were in for disappointment.

20

She soldiered on, and when my husband didn't show any reaction, she closed her notebook and walked upstairs to the spare bedroom turned studio. Tommy rose and followed. In less than half an hour, they were back downstairs. The art therapist gathered her purse and coat; Tommy headed back to the couch.

"See you next week?" I said, as I closed the door behind her. I looked at my husband, motionless on the couch, and doubted my words.

Tommy's arms were folded across his body. "How was your lesson?" I asked. No response. "Do you want to continue?"

Arms unfolded, two thumbs down.

"Not even one more try?"

He repeated the gesture.

"Okay," I sighed.

I called her and said, "It's not you; it's me. I was overly ambitious. Tommy just isn't into art therapy."

"Perhaps an hour?" she said. "We were too rushed."

"No, one of the effects of his illness is impatience." What I didn't add was, "Especially for art therapy that wasn't his idea in the first place."

I'm not sure why Tommy gave up on the painting he had labeled "a mess." And he can't explain why he rejected the art therapist. Or why, after she left the house, he rose from the couch and went back upstairs to work on *The Ice Cardinal*. Alone.

Perhaps my husband was saying he didn't want his wife to try to light his path with her bright ideas. And he didn't want a therapist to assist, no matter her expertise.

When Tommy was first doing paint by number, he likely enjoyed it because it was something he could do by himself, on his own schedule. As the degeneration progressed, perhaps he became frustrated when the last painting didn't compare to earlier ones.

So, maybe it was stubbornness that pushed Tommy back to the easel. He would show us. *The Ice Cardinal*, which he completed a bit at a time, has found its place on the kitchen wall. Soon, we'll have to scout a location for *Goldfinches*, his current paint by number.

Every night now, while Tommy is downstairs on his couch, in his prone position watching television and flipping channels, I slip upstairs to his studio and peek at this painting's progress. From the doorway, I see the beginning of a yellow bird, green leaves, and blue sky. No need for closer inspection. I raise two thumbs up and retreat.

Nine:
Easy Rider

I'm standing in the kitchen, looking out the back window toward the garage. My husband has just removed his Schwinn from where it rests in the corner. He crowns his head with a bicycle helmet and adjusts the strap. Then he releases the kickstand, mounts, and pedals off. He has left the garage door open.

I'm not upset at this gaffe, because he is wearing his helmet and has remembered to take his cell phone, notepad, and golf-size pencil. They are gone from the counter where he usually keeps them—a good sign.

I'm vigilant this morning because yesterday, when I was unaware, he rode off, leaving the helmet on a hook in the garage and the phone, pad, and pencil on the counter. And, instead of protective covering, he was wearing a baseball cap topped with AM/FM radio headphones.

When he returned from that bareback ride, he entered the house and was still adjusting the volume on his headphones when I blocked his path. I stretched my arms to grab his two shoulders. "Take them off and look at me," I said. "You can't hear when you have them on."

I didn't say this, but I thought, *Isn't it enough you can't talk? Why do you want to squelch another of your senses?* I didn't voice this because we avoid discussing his condition.

I reached up to remove one of his ear pads. He did the same on the other. "Honey," I said, looking straight at him so he couldn't miss my words, "you cannot, must not, wear these earphones when you're riding your bike. It's against the law." I don't know if this is true. In Tommy's case, it should be.

"You have to wear your helmet and take your cell phone and notepad with you." He nodded yes and started to put the radio earphones back on his head. "Remember, honey," I said, "if you should run into any problems on your ride, you need the notepad to tell someone to use your cell phone to call me." He put two thumbs up. He got it—I think.

Today, with all evidence showing he has heeded my words, I use the remote to close the garage door and head for the couch. I need a break. As I sink into the cushions, I recall the first time I saw Tommy on his bike. He wasn't wearing a helmet back then, but we were merely neighbors, not yet a couple. If I registered any problem with this risk, I must've have kept it to myself.

The year was 1996. I was separated from my husband of thirty years and had recently moved into a new townhouse on Henderson Street in Chicago. In the mornings, Tommy and I would wave, he on his bike, I walking my dog.

In the evenings, his wave turned into a pause at my gate to pet the dog. We'd chat a bit. Soon we became a twosome, and then, after my divorce, a married couple.

Throughout our fourteen-year marriage, Tommy continued to ride that old bike, until one day, when the garage door was left open, it was stolen. We replaced it with the Schwinn and added the helmet, lock, bell, and basket.

I wish I could send Tommy on the road as he was when we first met: a helmet-less, happy-go-lucky, assured rider. But I can't and I don't. I insist on the helmet, the cell phone, the pad, and the pencil.

These days, once he pedals off and clears the driveway—protected in the gear I count on—I make sure I close the garage door. Everything inside remains safe.

Ten:
Unpacking

My suitcase lies open and empty on the bed in our spare bedroom. Clothing, all black, to make wardrobe accessories easier, is in small stacks surrounding the bag.

It's been a year since my last trip to Boston to see my daughter Faith, and it was sixteen months earlier when I traveled to the West Coast to visit my other daughter, Jill. There was a point when I'd fly to either coast three times a year—often enough, I figured, that my grandchildren would know me in the flesh, not merely as an iChat image.

"Honey, I miss my kids" was how my trips typically began with my husband.

If the target were Boston, my husband would agree to join me because he liked the city's easy public transport that allowed us to tour on our own.

LA was another story. "Sun, golf," I'd offer.

"No, I'll stay home and take care of the dog,"

But the three-times-a-year timetable, and my husband's voiced responses to any trips, dissolved after his condition worsened. Today, Tommy can barely get a word out, communicating with clues written on Post-it notes.

"You've got to find some way to travel," Jill had said. "It's been over a year since you've been here. Look into home health agencies."

I did, and was relieved when Tommy didn't object to an aide

taking over for me one day a week. With her in place, I started to make plans for a four-day trip to Los Angeles.

Along with the aide, I enlisted our dog walker–house sitter to sleep over for the nights I'd be gone. Because she'd be at her job during the day, I asked two of my cousins to take Tommy to lunch a few times. My ex-husband said he'd visit on one of Tommy's unscheduled days. Neighbors volunteered to pop in and out. All were instructed to call me after their shifts, to let me know Tommy and the dog were okay and to convey Post-it-note questions.

I was covered. I bought airline tickets. I placed the suitcase and black wardrobe on the bed and added a bathing suit and sandals.

Several days before I was to fly from ORD to LAX, I called my daughter. "I'm worried," I said. "Tommy sometimes gags when he eats. I think it's a side effect of his condition. Something about the part of the brain that screws up his speech messes with swallowing."

"Mom, when did that start?" Jill asked.

I was embarrassed. "Actually, a few weeks ago," I said. "When I see it happening, I tell him to take small bites, put the fork down between mouthfuls. But now—"

My daughter interrupted, "Mom, you can't let him eat alone when you're gone."

I called the home health agency. "Can you send aides to monitor his mealtimes?" I asked.

"All set," I told my daughter.

Then I thought about it. I imagined Tommy confused in that whirlpool of caregivers. I worried, even with all those overseers in place—would one remind him to take his daily medications, especially the thyroid pills? Would another ask him to smile, as I do every morning, to be sure he'd inserted his dental bridge? And would another check the kitchen sink to make sure he'd turned off the faucets, and the front door to confirm he'd removed his keys from the lock?

And what if he was frightened and wanted me home?

"Canceling," I texted Jill.

"What happened?" she asked in the phone call that followed.

26

"I can't leave him," I said.

"I thought you had your team in place."

"I don't know what I was thinking," I said. "He could never handle it."

I could never handle it. I couldn't relax poolside in my bathing suit. I couldn't enjoy my grandsons' faces or antics. I couldn't devour time with my daughter. My head would be back in Chicago, worrying about my husband. I'd startle at the ping of a text or the ring of a cell, wondering if the news would calm or scare me.

The empty suitcase remains on the bed. Instead of returning the clothing to closets and dresser drawers, I'm plucking them one by one for my daily wardrobe. Eventually, only the empty suitcase will remain, and, for now, me.

Eleven:
Four Times Around

Tommy holds two hands in the air. Two fingers on each hand are raised. He uses one hand to draw a circle in front of him, as if he were twirling a lasso. He draws that circle twice. His face shines with sweat, and he is smiling.

"Four times around," I say. "That's two miles!"

He nods "yes."

My husband's first attempt to walk around the park for exercise, instead of riding his bike, is a success. This shouldn't surprise me; he used to be a runner.

"Half marathons," he said when we first met. He was sixty-one, muscled, with no visible fat, divorced, and a bachelor for fifteen years. I was fifty-eight, separated from my husband of thirty years, and on the lookout for a second.

Just a few months after our first hellos and a sweet romance, little by little, Tommy moved in with me. His exercise gear came first. Dozens of T-shirts, imprinted with running-event logos, scooted my Gap tees along the closet rod.

I relinquished one dresser drawer, then two, for his shorts, tank tops, and tube socks. And when his well-worn running shoes jumbled onto the closet floor, my high heels and sandals adjusted.

Once my divorce was final, Tommy and I married, and his workout stuff claimed permanent residency. Several years later, he stopped running. Plantar fasciitis, or some other pain in the bottom of his foot, ended it. To keep in shape, he switched to an elliptical machine at the local Y and, when weather permitted, rode his Schwinn.

I'm happy to see my husband continue to be active today. Although in some cases, primary progressive aphasia affects not only speech but also physical condition, perhaps Tommy's allegiance to fitness has deflected this symptom.

I thought I was doing well protecting my husband when he rides his bike by insisting he carry his cell phone, notepad, and golf-size pencil, but then I changed my mind. Tommy and I happened to be undressing for bed at the same time one night. Usually, I turn in two hours before him, but because we had returned home late from Passover dinner, he joined me upstairs.

He pulled off his sweater and an old running-event T-shirt he uses as an undershirt. When he started to shuck his slacks, I saw it: Tommy's body, still slim as the day we met, now bore a black-and-blue bruise. It was imprinted on his left thigh and resembled the shape of Italy: long, wide at one point, then narrowing.

"Tommy, what happened?" I asked. I ran my hand over the surface of the bruise, as if I were stroking a kitten. "Does it hurt?"

He shook his head "no."

"When did this happen?" No answer. This bruise could've been on my husband's thigh for days or weeks.

"Are you sure it doesn't hurt? I'll call the doctor in the morning," I said.

A head shake "no."

"Did it happen at the Y? Did you fall off the elliptical?"

Another head shake.

"Did you fall off your bike?"

A nod "yes." Bingo.

"When?" I sat down on the edge of the bed.

He took a pad and pencil from his nightstand—we have these all over the house—and wrote, "2."

"Two days ago? Why didn't you tell me?"

A shrug as he replaced the pad and pencil.

To me, the bruise appeared to be more ominous than a tumble off a bike.

"Were you hit by a car?" My heart was pounding.

Head shake "no."

Before I could continue, he got into his side of the bed, turned his back to me, and pulled the covers over his head.

"Honey," I said, loudly enough to penetrate his shield, "you have to take a break from bike riding until that bruise heals." I meant forever. "If you want exercise, how about walking around the park? Once around is half a mile."

Today, when Tommy returned from the park and triumphantly acted out his lasso routine, I breathed easier. After all, how much trouble can a fat-free former runner, banned bicyclist, and current walker get into as he strides four times around?

Twelve:
Food and Music—a Perfect Match

I'm not sure when he noticed me. Perhaps when I was opening Tommy's tiny ketchup pouch with my teeth, or when I put my hand on my husband's and said, "Slow," reminding him to chew one mouthful before taking another.

The stranger waited until we finished our lunch and Tommy was heading for the door before he stopped me and said, "I hope my wife takes such good care of me when I need it." I preened and thanked him.

This monitoring of my husband's meals is a new task in my caregiving routine. His PPA can also impact swallowing, so our mealtimes together have taken on a new, watchful ambience.

As Tommy and I left the restaurant to walk arm in arm, I thought about our very first meal together. Vigilance was absent back then. Our first date was at a Mexican restaurant that was walking distance from Tommy's apartment and my townhouse.

As we dipped corn chips into salsa, we revealed our favorite things. We were like game-show contestants hoping to find correct answers. We matched on *Masterpiece Theatre*, jazz vocalists, dogs and cats, and quiet nights at home. When we moved on from chips and salsa to tacos and burritos, our lists became more specific. And when we learned we had the very same favorite song, "It Never Entered My Mind," by Rodgers and Hart, we felt we had won first prize.

At my door after the meal, we exchanged a goodnight kiss,

31

neighborly, but with promise. Tommy said he'd call. I was certain he would.

The very next evening, instead of that phone call, he knocked on my door. "I have a present for you," he said.

We sat on the couch as I unwrapped a Johnny Hartman CD that included "It Never Entered My Mind."

"When, how?" I asked. I was touched.

"I took the El downtown and bought it at a music store," he said. "Do you like it?"

We played it then, and again at our wedding two years later, when my daughters walked me down the aisle in our Las Vegas ceremony.

While music has continued to be part of our lives, our meals have changed. Early on, we'd go to dinner once a week with friends. We'd argue over politics, discuss news headlines, catch each other up on far-flung children and grandchildren. When Tommy could still get a few words out, our dinner companions would try to keep him in the conversation. If necessary, I'd step in to translate.

Eventually, though, my husband could not speak at all. Our dinners out diminished because it became too painful for me to see him silent, on the sidelines. The invitations still came, but I accepted fewer and fewer, except for special occasions.

Tommy and I have compensated by upping our lunches out, just the two of us. Our fondness for food, just like our taste in music, is a perfect match. Hand in hand, one day a week, we go to Smoque, our favorite barbecue restaurant. On another day, we'll patronize Alps, a neighborhood Greek diner, and often we opt for Hot Doug's, the city's most popular hot-dog place.

My husband peruses menus with the pair of reading glasses I keep for him in my tote. He'll point to his choice, but I already know them: all of the vegetarian sides at the barbecue place, spaghetti with marinara at the diner, and a veggie dog with everything on it at the hot-dog joint. We share the fries.

On the afternoon when we arrived home from the barbecue place where I was praised for my caregiving, Tommy flopped on his couch to watch TV. I settled on mine and, since no

conversation would be forthcoming, put on my iPod headphones.
My musing about our first date at the Mexican restaurant, where
we matched on music, was still in my head. I scrolled through the
list until I found our favorite song, "It Never Entered My Mind":

I don't care if there's powder on my nose.
I don't care if my hairdo is in place.
I've lost the very meaning of repose.
I never put a mudpack on my face.
Oh, who'd have thought
that I'd walk in the daze now?
I never go to shows at night,
but just to matinees now.
I see the show
and home I go.
Once I laughed when I heard you saying
that I'd be playing solitaire,
uneasy in my easy chair.
It never entered my mind.
Once you told me I was mistaken,
that I'd awaken with the sun
and order orange juice for one.
It never entered my mind.
You have what I lack myself
and now I even have to scratch my back myself.
Once you warned me that if you scorned me
I'd sing the maiden's prayer again
and wish that you were there again
to get into my hair again.
It never entered my mind.

Thirteen:
Learning to Un-drive

Tommy and I were stalled in traffic; classical music was playing on the car radio. It seemed a good time to finally ask the question.

"Honey," I said, turning to my husband, silent in his passenger seat, "do you miss driving?"

That question had been a pest in my brain ever since I had taken away his car keys. I knew I had to force it out, place it before Tommy, if the guilt were ever to leave.

Needling in my conscience: How could I have deprived him of driving, of a skill he had worked so hard to accomplish? How could I have robbed him of his independence when so much had already been snatched away?

Tommy turned toward me, shook his head "no." Then he raised his hands and turned two thumbs down.

"You don't miss it?" I said. I wanted to be sure I understood his meaning. I wanted to be cleared of my crime, off the hook.

Another head shake "no."

I thought it ironic I was the one who had taken him off the road, when I was the one who had put him there.

It was 1999, the second year of our marriage. I was in the driver's seat; Tommy was a passenger because he didn't own a car, had no license.

"You've got to learn how to drive," I said. "I'm tired of doing all of the driving."

He was sixty-four at the time and took up the challenge as if he were a teen yearning for a shot at his dad's wheels.

After a series of lessons, Tommy got his license. I watched as he placed it in his wallet, tender and proud as a dad tucking his newborn in for the night.

For a time, we shared my car, but soon, like that teen he resembled, he wanted his own. To dealerships we went, inhaling new-car scents as we circled autos, debating exterior colors, interior upholstery, and the wisdom of a sunroof.

Finally, Tommy chose a champagne-colored sedan with power steering, power windows, a fob keychain that unlocked and relocked the doors, and cup holders.

"I love it!" he said, sitting upright in the driver's seat of his new car, hands at ten and two o'clock, as instructed. I was happy for him, and for me. I'd now have my car all to myself.

At the beginning, when we went out together, we used his car. We were like many married couples: husband in the driver's seat, wife a passenger reading the map, tuning the radio, or daydreaming out the side window. But after a while, I couldn't abide Tommy's driving.

"Red light, red light!" I'd shout, and stamp my foot on my imaginary brake.

"I see it, I see it!" he'd say, and we'd both bounce toward the windshield as the car came to an abrupt stop.

Eventually, I took the coward's way out. When Tommy was at the wheel, I'd settle into the passenger seat, close my eyes, and keep them shut until I heard the ignition turn off.

As the years passed—without me alongside harassing or zoning out—he started to have a few scrapes; then he got three red-light tickets in a row. And finally, the brain degeneration he was diagnosed with in 2009 slowly began to rob him of speech.

I worried, how could he explain himself to another driver if he were to have an accident? To a police officer? Neighbors who knew of his condition and had witnessed him leaving the scene of a fender bender worried about their young children. I insisted he stop driving.

Of course Tommy protested—who wouldn't? He surrendered

when I threatened to have his car battery removed. And when I promised I'd drive him whenever and wherever he wanted to go, he fished his keys from his pocket, held them in his fist for a second, then dropped them in my palm.

The following week we sold his car, the champagne-colored, full-featured, with sunroof, sedan he loved.

True to my word, I now drive my husband whenever, wherever. In my car, with me in the driver's seat and Tommy in the passenger's, I chauffeur him back and forth to the YMCA three days a week, to the golf store for putting practice, to drop-offs at the bowling alley or golf course to meet his buddies, to Home Depot or the garden shop for his supplies, and to doctor's appointments.

Although I once complained about being at the wheel full-time and I have now returned to that role, I'm not resentful. Tommy said he didn't miss driving. He repeated it with two thumbs down.

Fourteen:
Grateful He's a Tightwad

I'm in the audience of a medical conference on frontotemporal degeneration (FTD) and primary progressive aphasia (PPA), little-known illnesses for most, sadly familiar to me. The auditorium is filled with caregivers and members of the health care field.

Every since my husband was diagnosed in 2009, I've become well versed on the PPA version of the condition. But I figure there's always more to learn, so here I sit, hoping to catch news of some miracle cure.

I listen to speaker after speaker. Yes, awareness is building. Yes, research continues. But no, no hope yet for reversal of Tommy's loss of speech. I slump in my seat, discouraged.

A speaker steps onstage to introduce the topic of bvFTD. My attention sharpens; this version is new to me. I learn that the "bv" that precedes "FTD" stands for "behavior variant." Patients burdened with those added initials "can experience excessive spending with a lack of awareness of its implications," she says.

Then hands are raised in the audience, microphones are passed, and the horror stories begin—of loved ones' shoplifting, impulsive buying, and falling prey to Internet swindlers. "I came home and there was a boat in my driveway," says one caregiver, who has risen to her feet. The microphone goes to a man who volunteers, "She bought a new car, never discussed it with me."

I overhear a woman seated in my row say to someone on her

right, "My husband sent money to Nigerian scammers, and when I stopped it, they started harassing me."

And there was more: sweepstakes, mail orders, contests, door-to-door salespeople, lotteries—all spilled out as examples of bvFTD misery.

"My God," I say too loudly. To myself, I think, *Even if my husband could still talk or use computers, he'd never get bvFTD, because he's a tightwad.*

As I lean back in the cushioned seat, I recall a scene that supports my logic.

"I like it," Tommy said as he stared at the new Timex I had fastened on his wrist.

"You do?" I said. I stood back, hands on hips, and studied him as he twisted it upright so its white face was easily visible.

I was pleased at my husband's reaction, because this watch, which I had purchased at Nordstrom for $65, replaced the Pulsar he had worn for forty years.

Throughout our marriage, I had tried to get Tommy to give up that elderly timepiece. But he had always insisted on new batteries or fresh bands to keep it alive.

"Nope, this is dead" had been the last repairer's diagnosis.

"Please let me buy you another," I had said to Tommy. "I promise not to spend a lot."

The Pulsar wasn't the only long-held possession I've attempted to pry from my husband's hands and replace with a newer version. I'm still unsuccessful with his balding brown leather wallet.

"Look, honey," I say whenever we pass a display of billfolds. "This looks just like your old one. It's not expensive. How about it?"

He'll shake his head "no," put a hand on his pants leg to verify I haven't pickpocketed it, and pull my elbow to move me along.

Naturally, our differing views on spending money showed up early in our marriage. Although Tommy and I both grew up in households with little cash, my father was careless with his finances. I caught that gene and in my marriage to my first husband, a doctor, my lineage had a field day.

As for Tommy, paychecks were parceled out for necessities. He skipped college and went into the Air Force to help support his widowed mother. After the military, he worked to pay rent, utilities, and his YMCA membership and to build up a small savings account. No car, no credit cards, no up-to-the-minute fashions, no travels.

When we wed, I tried to spoil him with a joint checking account, a credit card, and a few doodads that I was happy to bestow on my penny-pinching husband. And while Tommy enjoyed these gifts, he never became infected with my loose-spending ways.

Now, as I sit in the auditorium, riveted by tales of depleted savings, unwanted merchandise, and giant credit card bills, I feel sympathy for those who cope with the wreckage left in bvFTD's wake.

For myself, I admit to new gratitude. True, no miracle cure awaits my husband, but his frugality, thus far, has kept us both from drowning.

Fifteen:
Take Care of Yourself

It's eight forty-five in the morning, and I'm at the living room window, watching my husband enter the passenger side of a car that is not mine.

The driver is an attractive young woman. In some other scenario, I'd be the jealous wife, tearful at Tommy's choice of a new companion. But since this is my life and the driver is my aide, my feelings are of relief, not wrath.

Hiring someone to spell me from full-time chauffeuring was sparked some months ago by directives from friends and relatives. "Be sure to take care of yourself," they said when they learned of my full-time responsibilities. Primary progressive aphasia, the brain degeneration that has shattered my husband's speech, has also changed me into his interpreter, advocate, and guardian.

To be honest, when I first heard that "take care of yourself" advice, I thought, *Easy for you to say.* That sounds petulant, I know, but I wondered how I could do that with my home and work responsibilities, our budget, and my stubborn spouse.

Then I had a second thought: *I deserve it.* So I decided if I could be untethered from driving—let's say, arrange a substitute for the three days I ferry my husband back and forth to the YMCA—I could count that as fulfilling my loved ones' order.

I went online and booked a taxi that would pick up Tommy at eight forty-five in the morning on Mondays, Wednesdays, and Fridays; drop him at the Y at nine; then return at eleven forty-five to get him from the coffee shop around the corner from the Y. I arranged a month of these round trips.

"Honey," I said on that day before my first day of Taking Care of Myself, "I'm going to a spa early tomorrow. A taxi will be outside at eight forty-five to drive you to the Y. Be sure to be downstairs."

"Okay," he said. He looked glum.

The next day, I left the house early. Tommy was still asleep, awaiting his own alarm. Off to the spa I went, first to get a massage, then to my locker to change for more pampering. As soon as I twirled the combination lock, I heard my iPhone ringing. This was not a welcome sound.

"Come home!" Tommy struggled to get out. (He still had words back then.) I looked at my watch; it was nine fifteen.

"What are you doing home?" I said. "Didn't the cab arrive to get you?"

"Come home!" he repeated. "The cab left!" This is what I figured: the cab arrived at eight forty-five, as ordered; Tommy was slow getting downstairs. The driver may have phoned the house, but Tommy didn't pick up. The driver left.

"I'll be there as fast as I can," I said. As I raced past the receptionist, I tossed, "Cancel my next appointment."

"No cabs!" Tommy said as soon as I walked in the door.

"No, no more cabs," I said. I went online and deleted the remainder of the taxi drives.

I returned to full-time chauffeuring until a few months later, I decided to try again, but not with a cabbie. And this time, I was less ambitious and sought only one day off, not three.

The job description I dictated to everyone I knew went something like this: "Wanted: male or female to spell me one day per week. Own auto essential. Medical background a plus. Patience a must."

Enter the attractive young woman who met all my requirements. When I first introduced this new chauffeur to my husband, he gave her two thumbs up.

Today, with Tommy's comely driver at the wheel, I've elected to use my three hours to stay home. I will not shower, nor put on makeup. I will dress in sweats, sans underwear. I will not leave the house or get into a car. I will not drive back and forth, back and forth. I will not watch over anyone but myself and the dog.

That's step one in Taking Care of Myself. For step two, I will go back online and schedule a taxicab to pick me up on a day my husband will be tucked in for a long morning nap. I will be downstairs on time and will give the cabbie—who is a driver that is not I—the address of the spa I abandoned. I will head to the receptionist's desk and once again book a massage, a manicure, and a pedicure. And as I luxuriate, I will pray that my iPhone keeps her mouth shut.

Sixteen:
Do You Have a Visual?

On the day my daughter and I were combing the aisles of Ocean State Job Lot, we weren't seeking the retailer's "quality brand-name merchandise at closeout prices." Instead, we were searching for Tommy.

"I don't have a visual," I shouted to Faith.

"Me neither," she said.

The tour of the forty-thousand-square-foot warehouse in Boston was Faith's idea to keep my husband and me entertained during our visit to her hometown. She knows Tommy is frugal, and thought he'd enjoy browsing. It was there I was teaching her an exercise I call "Find Tommy."

I don't think my husband deliberately tries to lose me. But now, during our trip, perhaps he had had enough of my hovering, my reminding, my suggesting, and had decided to give me the slip.

Even if Tommy was just teasing me with his disappearing act, I worried because his condition has left him vulnerable if he should get lost—hence my hunt.

At Job Lots, as Faith and I were midsearch, I shouted to her, "Check Pet Supplies."

"Nope," she called back.

"Weed and Feed Fertilizer?" my daughter yelled. She knows Tommy loves gardening, so that section seemed a good bet.

We threaded the aisles as if in a maze. Down through Household Cleaners, up through Bed Linens, past Golf Shirts, until I spotted his Red Sox baseball cap.

"Hi, honey," I said, as I latched onto his elbow. "Having fun?"

I gave no hint about the game Faith and I had just competed in. My husband is a proud, physically fit seventy-five-year-old who copes with his handicap bravely.

I, on the other hand, am often muddled.

Consider this incident that occurred on the day we were to attend a children's musical with my ten-year-old granddaughter in a major role.

"You must explore Jamaica Pond," Faith said on our first day as she dropped us off at our bed-and-breakfast lodgings. "Just turn left from your front door and cross the street at the light, and you'll be on the trail. It's a one-and-a-half-mile circle."

Tommy, who is a committed exerciser and regularly walks two miles around our neighborhood, brightened when he heard my daughter's suggestion.

Jamaica Pond is indeed a beautiful area, with sailboats lolling on the water, parents pushing strollers, athletes jogging, and dog owners tugging leashes. As soon as we dropped our suitcases in our room, my husband and I turned left from our front door and headed for the stoplight.

Before we reached the corner, Tommy started to cross. "Honey," I said, as I dragged him back, "look at these cars speeding by. You can't cross here. We have to go to the light." We didn't do the complete circle, just enough to give us a taste.

On the afternoon of my granddaughter's show—our primary reason for coming to town—I was relaxing on the bed, when I looked up to see Tommy lacing his gym shoes.

"Where are you going?" I asked. He pointed in the direction of the pond. "But I don't want to go," I said. "I'm resting."

He continued to point and indicated he was planning to leave without his hawkeyed wife.

"You can't go alone," I said. I jumped from the bed. This time, I had a visual: in my mind's eye, I saw him cross in the middle of the street. If he did make it to the other side, I pictured him lost. I envisioned a police search, a missed performance, and a daughter miffed at my messing up the evening.

But then I thought, *I'm overreacting. Maybe he* can *handle it.* I stuffed his pockets with the B and B's address, my business card, and his cell phone.

Then Tommy decided to shave. He used a Bic razor because he had forgotten to bring along his electric. When he emerged from the bathroom, his chin was bleeding. He was heading for the door.

"You're bleeding!" I said. "You can't go out like that."

I pulled him to the bed and applied Neosporin and a bandage. The words "What were you thinking?" suddenly slapped me. If Tommy didn't notice, or care, that he was bleeding, how could he travel safely on his own to the pond?

"I'll go with you," I said. I put on my gym shoes; we turned left at the front door, crossed the road at the light, and did a twenty-minute trek.

That evening, we had front-row seats. My eyes didn't leave my granddaughter for the entire musical. Well, maybe once or twice. He thought she was terrific, too.

Seventeen:
Green Thumb

It's six thirty in the morning, and I'm at the breakfast table, reading the newspaper, when my eyes veer from the print to catch the sunlight streaming in the window. Tommy, who is asleep upstairs, has raised the blinds to make room for seedlings he placed on the sill.

I leave my chair to read the tiny sticks stuck in the dirt. There are three TOMATO SUPER MARZANOS, two HABANERO HOT PEPPERS, one CAYENNE LONG SLIM HOT PEPPER, one SUPER CHILI HOT PEPPER, two CALIFORNIA WONDER BELL PEPPERS, and one CUCUMBER, PICKLING.

It was yesterday when my husband sped through the aisles of the garden center as I and a green-uniformed salesman followed. "Tomatoes," I called out behind me. "This way," the man said, and reversed our directions until we ended up in the proper row. And so it went with the rest of the plants now on the sill.

Tommy has had a green thumb as long as I've known him. When we first met, he was living on the second floor of a friend's two-story flat with a backyard and a garden. But because he worked a full-time job, he never had time to till that soil, plant, or reap.

When we married, in January 1998, outdoor gardening was out, so my new husband started with indoor plant maintenance.

"These need watering," he had said as he inspected my sorry potted plants. Moving along the dieffenbachia, schefflera, palm, and lily, he dug fingers deep into the soil and shook his head. He went to the kitchen, filled a pitcher with water, and, after dousing, asked for a rag to dust leaves. My plants perked up. I was grateful to have a custodian assume a role not in my DNA.

As soon as we moved into this house, with its big yard surrounded by fencing, Tommy surveyed his land and staked out plots for a vegetable garden. When Burpee catalogs arrived in the mail, I'd hand them over. He'd grab them as if they were letters from a long-lost relative.

Every day my husband would tend his garden. I'd watch as he inspected, watered, fertilized, and pampered. "Looking good!" I'd call out. He'd turn to my voice, wave a spade, and grin. "Not too long now," he'd say.

I'm not sure who was sunnier in those scenes: me, witnessing my husband revel in a simple hobby long awaited, or Tommy, blooming into a proud landowner.

When his crop yielded vegetables to rival a farmstand's inventory, he'd place half a dozen ripe tomatoes and several hot peppers in a plastic bag. "These are for the boys," he'd say, referring to his golfing buddies who savored his garden's output.

He'd stop neighbors. "I've got tomatoes, peppers, cucumbers, and potatoes," he'd say, looking as proud as a 4-H winner. "Want some?"

But this year, our idyll was threatened. When the seed catalogs arrived in the mail, I handed them to Tommy. Instead of snatching them, he pointed to the coffee table. I dropped them there.

Later, when I saw him stuff them, unopened, in the straw basket on the side of the couch, I asked, "Too much work?"

"Yes" was the nod. I wondered: Had the lapses in his brain that had ended his speech also turned his cherished pastime into something too complex? I didn't press him further.

Then something changed. It started with the cemetery. "Tommy," I said, "we have to get plants for my parents' graves." This was our annual Mother's Day ritual. We'd buy a few cubes of zinnia; pack a kit with a kneeling pad, a spade, a water bottle, and Wet-Naps; and head out to Waldheim.

At Home Depot, instead of stopping at the few posies for the graves, Tommy placed three hanging baskets and several flats of assorted flowers in his cart. "Front porch for the baskets?" I asked him. "Back-deck railings?" He nodded "yes." My heart lifted.

The next day I saw him heading out the door. "Where are you going?" I asked. Then I wrote, "Walk" and "Bike" on a Post-it. I waited for him to circle an answer. He shook his head "no" at each.

He took the pad and pencil and wrote, "Herb" under my two guesses. I knew what he meant. A landscape nursery was only a few blocks from our house.

"The garden center!" I said. "You're going to the garden center? Vegetables?" He nodded "yes."

"I'll go with you," I said, grabbing my sunglasses.

Soon, the plants that line the sill will be embedded in back-yard soil. My green-thumbed husband will water, tend, and reap vegetables for his buddies, our neighbors, and our table. We're keeping our fingers crossed.

Produce would be nice, too.

Eighteen:
The Screening Room

"Looks good!" says the speech pathologist. She is viewing an X-ray of my husband's head.

I'm watching the same picture. A second pathologist, on the other side of the wall, is giving Tommy instructions. He is compliant.

An apparatus is pointed at him as he swallows a spoonful of stuff. The viewer and I watch the screen as a snakelike strip wriggles unimpeded from his mouth to his throat and down into his esophagus.

"Next!" she calls out beyond the wall. The feeder nods her head. She dips a spoon into a plastic cup and offers my husband another dose of barium-laced food.

These doctors have assured me the amount of radiation used in this test is small and not harmful, and that it will take only about ten minutes. I am happy to hear this, because I can see Tommy is antsy.

"Are you comfortable?" the feeding pathologist asks my husband. He nods "yes" but soon rises from his chair to see what's going on behind our wall.

"No, no, sit down," the two doctors shout as the screen suddenly blanks.

He sits and then looks straight at the machine that is targeting his head. The feeder offers my husband another spoonful—thicker this time—while the viewer and I turn our focus back to the X-ray.

"Good," she says.

With each "good," my hopes rise. If Tommy gets all "goods," it will mean he, and I, will be saved from moving to a new, and unwelcome, path in caregiving. If he flunks this cookie-swallow test, I'll be directed to change his diet. I'll be forced to blend his food, monitor the consistency of each dish, and have someone at his side as he eats.

With each swallow, I tepee my hands in prayer because I also wish to keep my husband from sliding further down into the role of "patient."

This test was initially sparked by a conference for caregivers. When a nurse reported a case of choking, I thought, *Tommy sometimes coughs when he eats—is that choking?*

"Slow down" became my new command at the table. "One bite at a time," I'd say.

I tried to explain: "That condition that makes it hard for you to speak might mess with your swallowing. I don't want you to choke. Please chew and swallow before you take another bite."

In long-distance calls to my daughters, I confessed, "I hate this. It's taken all of the pleasure out of eating."

"Think of the alternative," they said. "Tommy choking, you trying the Heimlich, you panicking. Is that what you want?"

"No," I said. "I'll talk to his doctors."

Although they discounted the nurse's report and said they'd never heard of a patient choking, the doctors concurred a cookie-swallow test might be a good idea.

So here I am, watching feed, swallow, wriggle, smooth passage. As the spoonfuls proceed, I think about our mealtimes, which until recently had been a peaceful part of our day.

Ten years ago, beginning in 2002, Tommy and I tried vegetarianism. Our switch came after hearing friends credit their improved health and energy to their plant-based menus. And after we read *Diet for a Small Planet*, our own mantra became "nothing with a face" and "nothing that has a mother."

I lasted six months. A test for diabetes (it runs in my family) convinced me the amounts of carbs I'd been consuming—primarily pasta—put me at risk. And even when the results turned out to be false, I admitted I longed for forbidden foods.

Not Tommy. He has remained a vegetarian since his first bite of tofu. He never complains or envies me when I'm downing fried chicken or burgers. He happily eats his vegetarian meals, including those plucked from store freezers and microwaved.

"He did fine," says the speech pathologist. She is happy, too. My attention snaps back to the X-ray. "I don't see anything that would cause me to suggest a change of diet."

"His coughing?" I ask. "What about that?"

"Not a problem," she says. "In fact, tell him to clear his throat occasionally. That helps the food go down."

I race around the wall and grab my husband. "You passed, honey, you passed!" I say, elated as the parent of a Harvard grad.

That evening at the dinner table, Tommy and I indulge in a guilty pleasure we've enjoyed throughout our marriage: we disdain talk in favor of watching television.

Now, as we dig into our dishes—soy meatballs and spaghetti for Tommy, takeout rotisserie chicken for me—we fix our eyes on the set and a *Law & Order* rerun. The only words, the only commands, come from the screen.

Nineteen:
Toolshed

I use scissors to slit open the label covering the rigid plastic box. Once it's removed, I can unfold the top. The box is gray, tough looking, which is fitting for this Durabuilt 144-Piece Household Tool Kit.

Once the kit is spread open from the center, the box is exposed. It holds a wrench, pliers, scissors, a screwdriver, a hammer, and other tools, all packed in a convenient carrying case.

The case has a handle, but when I lifted it off the store shelf, I found it too heavy, so I cradled it in both arms and placed it in my shopping cart. My guilt felt as heavy as the tool kit.

Just two days earlier, I had made an offer to my neighbor John: "I'm on a mission to clean our basement and rid it of junk," I said. "Tommy has a wall full of dusty old tools he doesn't use. Would you be interested?"

"What do you want for them?" he asked.

"If you haul them out, along with all of the other clutter, they're yours."

Of course, I had asked Tommy first. "How do you feel about giving John the tools in the basement?" I said. "You've got enough in the kitchen cabinet for repairs. He plows our driveway in the winter; this would be a way of thanking him."

Tommy gave me two thumbs up. That was enough to give me clearance for full speed ahead on the de-shedding.

It was a different scenario when we first moved into this house, in 2000, two years after we were married. I was happy watching my new husband assemble his basement workroom. He mounted a pegboard on a wall, inserted hooks, and one by one attached tools he had accumulated over the years.

And he continued to buy more, often calling out to me, "Home Depot" as he rushed out the door. He'd return with just the right-size hammer, or perfect wrench, or saw, or some other needed implement.

I'd encourage him. "I need a shelf for my office," I'd say. "Can you do that?" Any project I could think of that would get Tommy down the stairs to gather materials would make us both happy.

The piles of wood that my husband accumulated—and that John eventually packed into the recycling can—were stockpiled during Tommy's alley trips. When we walked the dog, he'd pause at each opening, check to see if anyone had discarded wood, and, if so, change our direction until he had the lumber on his shoulder. On the route home, he looked like the leader of a Christmas procession.

On the day of the removal, John shouted up to me, "Come down and let me know if there's anything else you want out of here."

"Want to help us?" I asked my husband. He put two thumbs down, put on his radio headphones, and left the house for his afternoon walk around the park.

In the basement with John, I waved a hand across the wall of tools and pointed to lengths of twine, rope, extension cords looped on a hook; to dusty containers that held casters of various sizes; to plastic bags filled with bits of unknown origin. "All out," I said.

After John carted away the debris and left the house, Tommy returned from his walk. He opened the basement door and started down the stairs. I followed. At the foot of the stairs, we looked at the bare wall that had once held the pegboard and tools. We walked farther in and saw the basement, junk-free, with its remaining file boxes, golf equipment, gardening tools, and paint supplies stacked neatly on metal shelves.

Tommy's worktable was clean, except for the TV, cable box,

and tape player. He tried the devices; they were working properly. Before he turned to go back up the stairs, he stared at the blank wall. He made no gestures to tell me what he was thinking. No thumbs up or down. No Post-it notes with written clues. He just stared.

I put a hand on his arm and said, "Honey, when we go to Target this weekend, I'll buy you a new tool kit. Okay?" He put two thumbs up.

So that's what I did. Now the Durabuilt 144-Piece Household Tool Kit with "Ergonomic Grip, Wrench, Pliers, Scissors, Carrying Case, Screwdriver, and Hammer," which carries a "Lifetime Limited Manufacturer Warranty," sits open and waiting on the workshop's table.

I have to think of a project that needs Tommy's attention. A new pegboard might be a start.

Twenty:
All for One, One for All

It's a perfect day for golf. The sun is shining, and the temperature is in the seventies. There is no wind. Although I'm not a player, the weather delights me because it means Tommy will be hitting the links with his three friends.

This is Tuesday, the day of the week when I cede responsibility for Tommy to the group I call the Three Musketeers. I fancy Barry, Hal, and Marshall as characters from the Dumas novel, because the way they care for my husband means their motto must be "all for one, one for all."

I drive Tommy to the golf course and pay for his round and the rental of a pull cart. After he rolls his clubs onto the practice green, I take a seat on a concrete bench to await the arrival of at least one of the Musketeers.

While my love for the Musketeers could be considered self-serving because they give me a day off, Tommy enjoys their personalities; each player adds to their game a certain charm that keeps my husband entertained for hours.

Barry is the first to arrive. He is an artist, retired high school teacher, and devotee of dancing and jazz. "You're here!" Barry says as he approaches my bench. His golf bag is slung over one shoulder like artillery. Sometimes he can stop by our house to pick up my husband for their weekly outing, but today, other appointments interfered. "Don't worry, I'll bring him home," he always reminds me. All for one.

"Not a problem. I can drop him off," I tell Barry. I'm sincere. I enjoy this small respite on the concrete bench. I like seeing each Musketeer arrive from the parking lot. But mostly, I relish watching my husband on the putting green. His stroke looks perfect—careful, slow—as the ball slips through the grass and drops into the cup.

I never join the foursome on the course itself, so I can't ogle Tommy's swing. But I know he still lives by his mantra "hit 'em straight."

"He's still the best golfer in the bunch," Hal, aka Tiger, assures me. Hal is a retired advertising and sales promotion executive, which accounts for his proficiency as the Musketeers' organizer. He sets up tee times and starts the round of phone calls to alert the players. Hal's acted in local theater—a talent that surfaces when he narrates his latest joke.

The third Musketeer, Marshall, is a retired attorney. He's young at heart and the eternal optimist of the group. In Marshall's eyes, the glass is *always* half full, sometimes overflowing.

"Beats me every time," Marshall will tell me when I ask how their game went. Each Musketeer is aware I hang on to positive assessments. And a good game brings my husband home with a smile. When he opens the front door, his hand outstretched to show off his scorecard, his face is as bright as the morning sun.

There was a time when Tommy was obsessed with perfecting his golf game on his own, not only on Tuesdays. We bought the expensive cable package because it included the Golf Channel, he subscribed to two golf magazines, and there was never a question as to what he desired for gift-giving celebrations. "Book about golf," I'd tell my daughters when they queried. I'd purchase the same.

I encouraged this obsession. "Let's go online and search for DVDs," I'd say. Tommy, who shunned computers as if they were unexploded bombs, would pull up a chair next to mine. "That one," he'd say, as I scrolled the offerings. After the DVDs arrived, Tommy overcame his aversion and used my laptop as a screen.

There were memorable incidents during that time of my husband's addiction. Errant balls pinged a dent in the bedroom's sliding glass doors and in one of our living room windows. His determination to use real golf balls, instead of Wiffle balls, when he practiced at the nearby park would send me, a neighbor, and the park director to his spot. We pleaded with him to switch; he turned us all down.

This season, all practice in the house and park evaporated. We still have the Golf Channel, but Tommy lands on it only while flipping through stations with the remote. No new DVDs have been ordered. And when my daughters asked about Father's Day, my answer was, "Sweatshirt, no logo, medium."

I'm grateful my husband still relishes his Tuesdays with his Musketeers. That's when Barry, Hal, and Marshall watch over him and I take off. All for one, one for all. Cue La Marseillaise.

Twenty-One:
Softy

Tommy and I are on a subway platform in the Loop, waiting for the Blue Line to take us home. I'm leaning on a metal column and peering down the track to spot the headlights of the next westward-bound train.

My husband has positioned himself on the opposite side and selected his own pillar for support. His eyes are riveted on a pair of musicians a few feet from me. The male plays a guitar and the woman sings—a Spanish song, quite lovely, and a nice respite from the clang of trains and chatter of waiting passengers.

An open guitar case is at their feet. Some paper bills are already strewn inside from earlier donors, and perhaps the duo has seeded the case to encourage more.

I leave my train watching to focus on my husband. I stare as his hand reaches into his pocket. I knew this would be coming. His eyes are misting as he pulls out his wallet and extracts a bill, which I'm hoping is $1. He drops it into the guitar case, and the duo nod a *gracias* in his direction.

"Musicians are okay," I had told him earlier. "But the panhandlers on the corners are scam artists." I believe this is true, for I've seen one on crutches suddenly able-bodied and sauntering from his spot near our house.

My husband obeys this rule. As long as he can drop a bill into a musician's case, he's a happy philanthropist.

Since I didn't know Tommy in his younger days, I can't attest to his generosity back then. But, because he's always been frugal, I'm assuming he wasn't so quick on the draw with street musicians and beggars.

I could be wrong, but I think the new largesse is part of his current condition. The frontal lobe of the brain affects emotions, and ever since his began to deteriorate, he's become a softy. Along with his charity, he's a weeper at sad and happy television shows, and at bar mitzvahs and weddings.

When my husband begins to tear up, the celebration hosts are touched. "Such a sensitive man," I imagine they whisper to one another.

I've done a lot of reading about Tommy's condition and am relieved to learn he has not taken on another emotion that is sometimes linked to the illness: rage. If anything, he has become kinder (witness the charity), more sentimental (the tears), and softer.

Because he can no longer speak, he doesn't send irritating comments to television commercials, obese strangers, or other innocent targets, as I once complained about. I understand now those slurs were the beginning of his brain's degeneration—inappropriate responses are a classic symptom. I haven't explored whether these barbs are still in his head; I prefer to think he no longer holds them.

Today in the subway, I say to Tommy, "Please show me what you gave the musicians." He opens his wallet and points to a $1 bill. "Good," I say. "Now be sure to tuck your wallet deep in your pocket." He does, and then pats it for emphasis.

At the end of the line, when we have descended the stairs, a disheveled beggar is at the stoplight near the expressway. He is holding a sign—HOMELESS. NEED FOOD.—and is limping toward cars that are stopped and waiting for the light to change.

I turn to look at my husband. I see his hand reach for his pocket. "Tommy," I say. He looks at me, nods his head, and drops his arm at his side. I take his hand in mine as we cross at the WALK sign. My husband glances back and watches the guy continue to hobble dramatically along the cars.

"Fake," I remind Tommy. He nods his head in agreement. When we reach the other side, I look back and send a silent suggestion to the grifter: *Should've hummed a few bars.*

Twenty-Two:
Crime Scene Investigation: Chicago

It was like an episode of *CSI* when the team prepared to search a Dumpster for some vital clue. I was pulling on a pair of white vinyl exam gloves—latex free, powder free—and smoothing each finger so the glove would hug each digit.

I used an empty plastic garbage bag to hold the contents of our tall kitchen trash can. Unlike the TV investigators who seek elements of a crime, I was hunting for Tommy's lost keys.

The receptacle was an inspiration and my last hope. My husband and I had already yanked all the pockets of his clothing inside-out. Had already peered under the bed, under the nightstand, under the couch cushions, under the couch. When all of these turned up empty, a dark thought entered my head: *Tommy must have left them in the front door, and some miscreant absconded with them.*

So I decided to change our morning's plans. "We'll go to Sunday breakfast," I told my husband, "but instead of continuing on to do our banking and our grocery shopping, we'll come home straight away. I'll call a locksmith then." He gave my plan two thumbs up.

As a devotee of all crime shows, I figured that whoever purloined the keys would be watching our house and would burglarize it the minute we left. So, after exiting the driveway, we drove around the block and crept back home. Since nothing was amiss, we proceeded to a nearby diner.

I raced through my egg-white omelet with thoughts of my iMac and iPad being lifted from the house and piled into a white van with the misleading logo of a repair company. "Finish your coffee," I said to my husband. I was already standing and packing up. "We've got to get home."

No white van was parked in front of our house. Inside, my Apple products were safely tucked in their spots. Nothing had been disturbed. Still, I called a locksmith. While waiting for a callback, I decided to Dumpster-dive.

One by one, I plucked. Gingerly. First, I lifted out a white, cone-shaped coffee filter filled with the morning's Trader Joe's French roast. Next, crumpled paper towels that earlier had held an ice pack used to soothe my aching back. Onward to dust and dirt swept up from the kitchen floor. Finally, I drew out several tiny foils that had once been wrapped around miniature chocolate candies.

And there they were: Tommy's keys, staring up at me as if to say, *Ta-da!*

First, I canceled the locksmith. Then, dangling the keys, I raced upstairs to our bedroom, where my husband had not given up the search. "Look," I said. "I found them! They were in the garbage." He grasped the keys, smiled, and plunged his fist with the treasure deep inside his pocket.

This is what I figured happened: Tommy left our neighborhood block party before I did. He let himself into the house and removed his keys from the lock but kept them in his hand. Then he went straight to the freezer, plucked a candy from the door's shelf, unwrapped it, and tossed foil and keys into the garbage.

I could ascribe Tommy's lapse to his illness, but then a list of my follies—and that of my two daughters—popped into my brain. Once, I left my fully loaded backpack on the floor of a local McDonald's—overnight. Fortunately, the manager spotted the bag and held it for me until I came for it the next morning.

Another time, I left my wallet on the counter at Trader Joe's. I didn't discover my loss until I returned home to put away my receipt. An eagle-eyed employee had spotted it and kept it safe until I returned within the hour to retrieve it.

I remembered Faith's story of leaving her MacBook on a seat at the boarding gate and not remembering it until she was belted in. A plea to the flight attendant miraculously won her an escape to pick it up exactly where she had left it.

And Jill left her MacBook Air still charging at her sister's house after she had hugged good-bye and departed for Los Angeles. Federal Express brought it home to her within two days.

I relate these tales—you are likely already contributing your own lost and misplaced examples—to emphasize that sometimes, missing objects are not a result of some sort of theft but instead just a case of plain old absentmindedness. Nothing more.

Twenty-Three:
When the Caregiver Needs Care

So, I'm on the appliance store's website and thinking the five-cubic-foot Frigidaire White Chest Freezer, at $197, might be a good idea. I could fill it with the pack of four Palermo pizzas I spotted at Costco, and with dozens of packages of the frozen vegetarian dinners that my husband likes. That way, when I go to the hospital for two days, and when I'm home thumping around on crutches, or with a cane, or pushing a walker, Tommy can possibly prepare meals.

My hip-replacement surgery is scheduled for September 20, eight months after two orthopedic specialists said, "You're limping. It's not your back; it's your hip." X-rays verified arthritis had eroded the cartilage in my right hip and the spooky "bone on bone" was the culprit.

"Do it sooner rather than later," my neighbor, a physical therapist, advised. Others chimed in with supportive quotes like "Wish I had done it ten years earlier" and "I feel like a teenager again."

But thoughts of any surgery, hospitalization, and rehab bumped up against my caregiving responsibilities. How would my husband fare if I had to be gone from him overnight? How would he continue his three-times-a-week exercise routine at the Y if I couldn't drive for at least four weeks? Laundry, grocery shopping, and this and that kept me postponing a visit to a surgeon.

When I admitted I could no longer walk even once around

our neighborhood park, I booked the appointment that led to the scheduled date. The surgeon concurred, "If medication and injections no longer work, surgery is the only option to relieve the pain and get you walking easily again." He penciled me into his hospital schedule, gave me instructions for the interim (continue my cautious workout routine), and told me his nurse would be in touch. My planning began.

I alerted dozens of relatives, neighbors, and friends to my due date. Their responses—"I can help"; "Count on me"; "Whatever you need"—eased my mind. And when I told my husband the September date and assured him his routines would continue unabated, he gave me two thumbs up.

I relaxed even more when I replayed a scene in my head. It was the first meal Tommy made for me after we met.

"This is lovely," I remember saying as I toured his place. I thought he must have spent time tidying it up for my visit, but now, after having been married to him since 1998, I realize he's an orderly person and his apartment was likely untouched.

Tommy was smitten with me back then—I have letters and notes to prove it. "Sit here," he said, pulling out a dining room chair slowly so it wouldn't scrape or shriek. There was a place mat, I'm sure, and silverware on one side of a dinner plate. (I have since demonstrated how they are separated: fork to the left, knife and spoon on the right.)

Our meal was broiled chicken, cooked squash, and . . . What was the starch? I can't recall. But I so remember the squash because I have replicated his recipe many times since then (brown sugar stirred into the defrosted and cooked block).

The other thing that sticks in my memory of my bachelor Tommy was his Friday nights at the Laundromat. As he described his weekly routine to me, I could see my middle-aged swain sitting on a chair next to an empty shopping cart, a paperback mystery in his hands, one load of his laundry soaking and spinning.

When he moved in with me, just a few months after the chicken-and-squash dinner, I took him by his hand to my washer and drier. "No more Laundromats," I said. I was happy to declare this.

"Terrific," he said, as he put his arm around my waist and kissed my cheek.

So why am I stressing? My husband can no longer speak, but he can certainly cook a frozen pizza and place an Amy's fake-meatloaf dinner in the microwave. And, although Tommy hasn't had to tumble a load for fourteen years, I bet he could follow the instructions permanently imprinted on the inside covers of the Whirlpools.

If I purchase the extra freezer, I could include several blocks of squash in the inventory. My husband's memory is intact; I'm certain he'll remember the recipe. Brown sugar is the key.

Twenty-Four:
The Turnaround Tango

It's 5:00 p.m., and the dance my husband and I perform daily—which I have dubbed the Turnaround Tango—is about to begin. Music would be nice, but our duet is staged in silence.

I'm in the kitchen, preparing dinner. A pot of spaghetti is nearing its boil on the stove. I remove a colander from its place in a cabinet and set it in the sink. When the timer rings, signaling al dente, I lift the pot by its two handles and turn around to dump pasta and water into said colander. Alas, the pockmarked utensil has vanished.

In his fancy step, while my back was turned, Tommy has removed the colander from the sink, placed it back in the cabinet, and exited. He has not done this to vex me; this I know. He just can't help it.

I remain standing—a tricky move because I am holding the cauldron with padded gloves, steam is clouding my eyeglasses, and I have nowhere to toss its contents. I hold this pose for a beat, then swivel and return the steaming pot of spaghetti to the stove.

Early on, when I first encountered my husband's stealth moves, I would try this: "Honey," I'd say, "please come back into the kitchen and get the colander out of the cabinet where you put it. I need to drain the spaghetti."

Tommy would return, a contrite grin on his face, and perform his well-practiced steps. But I no longer make that request. I have memorized my moves: button lip, pot back to stove, retrieve colander, return to sink, lift pot, and dump.

Our Turnaround Tango takes place in other areas of our house and at various hours. A pantry door opened to extract garlic and Italian spices is closed before I get out the first dash; same for the refrigerator when soymilk is used for my Cheerios. Ditto for the garbage can lid I keep open while doing kitchen prep.

The reporter notebooks I use for Trader Joe's and Target shopping lists are invariably returned to a neat stack after I have separated them and laid them side by side for easy entries. All it takes to cue my spouse is for me to turn my back.

"Don't you get mad?" a friend asked. "Don't you want to scream at him? Tell him to leave your stuff alone?"

I answer, "I think it helps Tommy when I remain calm." I believe this to be true. My husband shows no rage in dealing with his illness.

To this friend, who has had her own frustration with a stubborn, aging relative, I say, "I'm a patient person. This comes naturally to me."

But I fear I lie. I can recall many instances when I am anything but patient. See me drumming the table of a restaurant until the waiter comes for our order. That's me at the hot-dog stand, stewing, while the proprietor chats it up with the customer in the front of the line. And, yes, that's me fuming in any and all medical offices while waiting for my name to be called.

So, how am I able to remain saintly with my husband? What good would it do to seethe or explode? His condition prevents him from veering from his compulsive, neat-making routine. The pattern of his dance steps is imprinted on his brain; he cannot do otherwise.

As for me, petite and compact, I'm quick on my feet. Over the years, I've been able to practice my moves. Sometimes I stumble if the steps are too difficult. Often I wish I could get one maneuver down perfectly before another is introduced into our lives.

Thus far, I've kept up with my creative dance partner. The trick is to let him lead.

Twenty-Five:
The Kids Are All Right

Tommy and I have just expanded our family: a boy and a girl. They arrived not as bundles from heaven, but in a Jeep and on a bicycle. In truth, they are young-adult occasional companions for my husband—miracles of referrals, rather than biology or science—whom I've hired to give me respite from round-the-clock caregiving.

I do have flesh-and-blood daughters. But since they live far away, they can't be at our beck and call. As for Tommy, he entered this second marriage sans children—hence my designation of this new, adopted duo as "our kids."

Before our boy, Stuart, came for his first assignment, I prepped my husband. Unlike the cinematic moment "Darling, I have wonderful news. You're going to be a father," my revelation went something like this: "Honey," I said, "I've hired a young man who will take over driving you to the Y one day a week. He's a CNA— that's certified nursing assistant—so he can also help out when I have my hip-replacement surgery."

Well, okay, I fudged a bit. Stuart's medical credentials are important for Tommy's condition, but I hesitate to remind my husband of his special needs. I can take the fall—metaphorically, of course, because of the hip thing—as I really do see our boy being helpful when I'm shouting for my crutches.

After Tommy gave the plan two thumbs up, I gave Stuart this checklist: "Before you leave the house, be sure Tommy takes his reading glasses, cell phone, and gym bag, and that he's wearing his dental bridge, baseball cap, and gym shoes." Stuart—using an impressive two-thumbs entry—recorded it all on his iPhone, immediately winning me over with the product and the pace.

On the morning of their first drive, I left for the health club at six o'clock. Stuart would use his own new key to gain entry at eight thirty. "Don't text me unless there's a problem," I told him, though that didn't keep me from checking my own iPhone at eight thirty, eight forty-five, and nine. Nada. I was at peace.

Tommy and Stuart were due back between eleven forty-five and noon. After a sublime four hours to myself, I returned home to await their arrival. At 11:40 I stationed myself at our picture window and watched as each car turned the corner onto our street. At exactly eleven forty-five, a black Jeep entered my view.

"Everything was fine," Stuart said as Tommy walked into the house with two thumbs raised. "He was all set when I arrived, everything on the checklist completed." I felt as proud of them as if they had just aced their ACTs.

Our girl, Kristen, had been engaged to be my husband's companion one afternoon a week. Her task was to follow him as he rode his bicycle to a park about a mile away and then circled the grounds four times before heading back home. Ever since Tommy had returned from a ride with the unexplained bruise on his leg, I had worried about his safety.

For her first shift, Kristen rolled up to our house outfitted in a gingham summer dress over bike shorts. She wore a helmet and, slung across her body, an enormous leather purse, which I later insisted she forgo in favor of one of my archived backpacks.

I had told Tommy about Kristen's arrival and again employed the hip excuse. "I won't be able to drive for at least four weeks," I said. "Kristen can keep you company on bike rides or use our car to take you to the putting green, the golf store, or wherever you want to go."

But I needn't have dissembled, because the moment Kristen—who is an actress—removed her helmet, shook out her hair, and smiled, my husband rushed to the garage to get his bike. While this duo was on their ride, I once again peeked at my iPhone, willing away any text messages. I was thankful when, as with Kristen's faux sibling, none arrived. And a little over an hour from the time they'd left, the two returned.

"It was fine," Kristen said. "I followed behind him"—they used sidewalks—"and alerted people as we approached. We stopped for water, then headed home."

Tommy, his face moist and smiling, gave her two thumbs up as he headed for the couch. Before she left, Kristen went to where Tommy was prone to say good-bye. Instead of shaking his hand, she dotted his damp forehead with a kiss.

Perhaps the kids *are* heaven-sent after all.

Twenty-Six:
Better Late Than Never

When Tommy returned from his trip to Walgreens, he was carrying a plastic bag that appeared to contain more than the AAA batteries he had gone to purchase. From the square shape of the box within, I thought it to be golf balls.

"What did you get?" I asked. I was teasing, for no matter how many dozens he has stored on basement shelves, I don't mind his adding to his collection.

My husband smiled and entered the house, leaving me on the porch, where I had stationed myself to enjoy a beautiful Saturday afternoon. But, after spilling coffee on a garden chair, I left my spot to get cleanup equipment.

I spotted the square box on the kitchen counter. Instead of a package of golf balls, as I had guessed, the box was yellow, trimmed in gold, and decorated with familiar red flowers, a green border, and the words "Whitman's Sampler" in green lettering. A yellow envelope addressed to me lay next to it. I opened the card that read, "Happy Birthday from the Group!"

"Thank you, sweetheart!" I called out as I searched for Tommy. I found him installing the new batteries in his headphones and acting as if there were no surprise waiting for me.

"I love the card and the chocolates!" I said, as I pulled him from his task.

My husband's eyes moistened. He placed the AAAs and headphones on the counter and bent down to accept my kiss.

Then he picked up his equipment and returned, smiling, to finish his job.

Although my birthday had been the previous week and "from the Group" was a bit off base, I was thrilled to receive both the card and the gift. Tommy had remembered after all. I know he chose this particular card, rather than a more appropriate "To My Wife," because at Walgreens he didn't have his reading glasses with him, and this card's "Happy Birthday" was large, colorful, and easy to spot. He didn't sign it, but no matter. I knew the identity of my gift giver.

On August 10, the morning of my actual birthday, when the kitchen counter had been vacant of card or chocolates, I hadn't been hurt or angry. I knew if my husband could have pulled it together, he would have. On past birthdays, I could count on a sentimental "To My Wife" card and a bouquet of flowers greeting me in the morning. But since Tommy no longer drives, I realize that would have been difficult.

I'm certain he knew the actual date because phone calls wishing me happy birthday started early that morning and cards that arrived in the mail were displayed on our dining room table, along with a basket of treats my daughters had sent.

Because I thought his lapse on my special day was due to his inability to purchase something on his own, I had an idea. When his Friday driver, Stuart, came to pick up Tommy, I made this suggestion: "There's a Hallmark next to the coffee shop where you get Tommy," I said. "Tell him you saw on Facebook that it was my birthday and would he like to stop in and get a card."

"No problem," Stuart said. But when the two arrived home and my husband led the way inside with only his gym bag, I looked at Stuart for clues. "I asked him," he whispered to me, "but he made it clear he wanted to go straight home."

Since Walgreens is only a block from our house and Tommy's language problems don't prevent him from making an off-the-shelf purchase, he could have bought the card and chocolates on my actual birthday. And Stuart did give him the option to buy something that same day. My husband chose neither.

I have a theory about why he picked today—eight days after

the fact. I believe he wanted to separate himself from the crowd—make his gift and card more special than the rest. He wanted to let me know he cared more for me than anyone else, more than the first-thing-in-the-morning well-wishers or card and gift senders.

Anyway, that's what I think. It doesn't really matter. The greeting card "From the Group" is propped on its own on the dining room table, and every bite of candy feels like love.

Twenty-Seven:
Tommy Untucked

"Are you sure you want me to buy these?" I asked Tommy as we stood in the candy aisle at Target. In one hand, I was holding a 10.5-ounce bag of mini–Three Musketeers, Milky Ways, Trix, and Snickers, and in the other, a 12-ounce mini–Hershey's with Nuggets.

As I waited for my husband's response, my eyes landed on his tummy, which lately has plumped and oozed over his belt.

Ignoring my stare, Tommy answered with two thumbs up.

I persisted. "These candies are making you gain weight." I said and shook each bag for emphasis. "You're eating too many of them."

He continued his affirmative thumb raise.

"Okay," I said, as I tossed the bags into the cart and rolled on.

My seventy-seven-year-old husband is dealing with a serious medical condition that has robbed him of speech and dimmed his reasoning. How can I deny him sweets? Also, he is stubborn and likely wouldn't listen to any lectures on wise food choices.

But as I pushed the cart through the aisles and Tommy headed up the escalator to savor golf equipment, I thought of the man I'd married fourteen years earlier. He was a proud 145 pounds, with nary an ounce of pinchable fat. His biceps were as solid as Major League baseballs, his calf muscles sloped impressively upward, and his stomach was enviously flat.

This physique was hard-won. "I was a smoker and overweight," he confessed in the dawning days of our romance. "My cholesterol was high, and I was in lousy shape. When the doctor told me I had to change my lifestyle or I'd die, I did what he said."

So Tommy joined the local YMCA and became a regular. He stopped smoking, started running and bike riding, and in time dropped weight and lowered his blood pressure and cholesterol.

On top of that, he's judicious about his portions of meat-, chicken-, and fish-free meals and appears to stop eating when full. But he can't seem to resist those mini-chocolates.

Throughout the day, I see him rise from his prone position on the couch, or return from a bike ride or park walk, and head for the kitchen. I hear the familiar gasp of the opened freezer door, the crinkle of a plastic bag, then the slap of the sealed door. Next, the pop of the garbage can lid, the rip of foil, and the sugary symphony's final note as the lid slams shut.

I finally decided one day that if I couldn't stop Tommy from gorging on the minis, I could do something to improve his appearance and ease.

He was on the couch with the TV remote, flipping through channels. As always, his T-shirt was tucked into his size-36 cargo shorts, and a black leather belt looped around and clasped the waistband. His paunch loomed over the belt, which didn't disguise the freed first button.

"Why not remove the belt and untuck your shirt?" I said. "You'll be much more comfortable."

I didn't wait for his answer. I unhooked the belt from its notch and wrenched it out like a whip. Then I wrestled his T-shirt, with its Free Spirit Japanese imprint, out of his shorts and draped it over his stomach.

"Now, stand up, honey," I said. "Isn't that better?"

He rose, gave a deep breath, put two thumbs up, and did a little shimmy shake, which I took as two degrees above the thumb raise.

"You look nicer, too," I said. "Slimmer."

He grinned and did one more dance before returning to the couch and MeTV.

Now that he's untucked and his belly is hard to spot, I ignore his jaunts to the freezer. Let him enjoy. There are always size 38s, elastic waistbands, sweatpants, and other wardrobe fixes that will allow my husband to expand.

At his next exam, when his cholesterol and blood pressure are checked, it will be up to his doctor to discover whether the levels have risen, and perhaps to issue a warning. But since she knows Tommy's diagnosis and is aware of his losses and day-to-day struggles, I suspect her prescription will be similar to mine: "Enjoy," she'll say.

And he will.

Twenty-Eight:
Prince Charming

Tommy is on bended knee before me, holding a Capezio ballet slipper in one hand. We are both laughing. The scene reminds me of Prince Charming when he finds his Cinderella and the perfect foot to fit the glass slipper.

Our mirth doesn't exactly match the fairy tale but instead is the result of my husband's attempts to figure out where to put the elastic strap that crosses the instep on the shoes I use as house slippers.

"No, honey, my foot goes *under* the strap and into the shoe," I tell him as I put a hand on his shoulder to steady myself. But Tommy insists on putting the band on my heel.

I am unfazed; we have several days left to practice. I'm readying Tommy to help me when I return from hip-replacement surgery and am not allowed to bend over to put on my own shoes. He is eager to show me he can come through for me.

Earlier that day at lunch, I deliberately dropped a napkin on the floor. "This is a rehearsal," I said. "Can you pick up the napkin for me?" He did, with a grin. He was enjoying this gallant role.

My tests continued throughout the day. "Give me your elbow, please," I said, realizing this trial needn't wait until post-surgery, because my arthritic hip had already made me a hobbler. "And walk slower, honey—I can't move this fast." He complied and, like an escort leading an elderly patron to the opera, moved one foot at a time.

At home, it was this request: "Keep your eyes on me as I walk up the stairs, just in case I topple backward." Instead of viewing my assent from his spot on the couch, my Prince Charming rose and stood at the base of the stairs. He watched as I slowly practiced the step-by-step instructions in my presurgery pamphlet.

When I reached the top of the stairs, Tommy returned to the couch and his TV program. That was fine with me; he had completed enough tests to assure me he'd be a competent caregiver. And if I needed further evidence of his empathy for the ill, all I had to do was recall an incident with an ailing uncle that convinced me Tommy would be a good mate.

My uncle Nate was in a residential facility, suffering from Parkinson's and psychosis. It was no longer safe for him to be at home. Tommy and I weren't married, just mature sweethearts, when he accompanied me for a visit. As soon as they were introduced, Tommy said to my uncle, "Would you like to take a walk?" Then he hooked elbows and slowly ambled along the hallway with Uncle Nate.

As I watched the two men—one a treasured figure from my childhood, the other a second-husband prospect—I realized how important this trait would be in my life. Tommy would be someone I could count on to care for me when the need arose.

As it turned out, Tommy beat me to it. I've been the one wearing the caregiver's cap. But I know that if the situation were reversed, if I were the one suffering a variety of losses, my husband would not leave my side or protest his new responsibility.

So, we're about to have a real-life test, albeit a temporary one. I'll be in the hospital for two days (I pray), then home for rehab for three to six weeks. Friends, relatives, and neighbors will be around to assist us both.

But there will be times during my return to physical health that it will be just my husband and me. While Tommy is silent in his requests, mine will be loud and insistent: "I want my cane," I can hear myself saying. Or "Please put a load in the laundry so it doesn't pile up." Perhaps "Can you start dinner? Make salads? Set the table?" All new language of need from yours truly.

I've been fortunate, in the years we've been together, to have been a healthy woman—no previous hospitalizations and no memorable cold or flu happened that required Tommy's attentiveness. If they did, he evidently brought me the requested medicine, bucket, or hot broth, or I would remember his lapse. Wouldn't I?

I am certain that in this upcoming episode in our lives, Tommy will turn out to be a caregiver extraordinaire, and soon enough he will figure out the Capezios. Tending to his Cinderella will soon be old hat for my Prince Charming.

Twenty-Nine:
How to Suction a Tracheotomy

My last blog post was September 18, 2012, two days before I was to undergo a total hip replacement. That was a lifetime ago.

Today, more than a month later, my hip is nearly repaired and I am back to driving and usual activities. Sadly, tragically, those activities now include caring for my husband at home, with hospice as support.

We have been through an unbelievable nightmare, with my dear Tommy suffering more than anyone else. It all started with swallowing. For several months, he had to be reminded to chew one mouthful before taking another. Then that routine started to deteriorate, until he could not swallow anything. He took in, then spat out, sips of water or Gatorade.

Dehydration was also a worry. One evening, when I was already upstairs, I heard a thump. I ran down, and at the foot of the stairs was my husband, awake, unhurt, but seeming to wonder what had happened to him.

The following morning, Stuart—the certified nursing assistant who had been driving Tommy to the YMCA several days a week—and I took him to Northwestern Memorial Hospital's ER. He was admitted with severe dehydration. Because Tommy could not swallow—which we all assumed was a symptom of his PPA—the ENT team recommended a tracheotomy (lest he smother) and a feeding tube for nourishment.

This is the part where the nightmare became so dark and

frightening that we prayed it was indeed something happening in our sleep. But it was not to be; it continued when we were awake. When the ENT team attempted to insert a tube through Tommy's mouth and into his stomach, they encountered a blockage, a mass. Doctor's diagnosis: "Squamous cell carcinoma of supraglottis. You are not a candidate for treatment for this cancer." Throat cancer. Aggressive.

Our decision was to bring him home to hospice care, where he could be kept as comfortable as possible.

After ten days in the hospital, on October 21, we returned via ambulance to our house in Independence Park. Several neighbors had already been on board to assist with equipment delivery and to get Tommy all set up in our bedroom. Other neighbors wrote their phone numbers on slips of paper with the words "Anytime, 24 hours."

Now, my husband is hooked up to balky machines that provide oxygen and humidity with a tube that goes directly into his tracheotomy. Every few hours he coughs, alerting me and a CNA, Rebecca, or other round-the-clock caregivers that his trach is accumulating mucus and secretions and making it difficult for him to breathe. That's where the suctioning comes in. I watched the hospital nurses perform the procedure, studied a YouTube video, assisted Rebecca with her first suction, and then, miraculously, did the "cleanse, insert, twist, suction, and extraction" on my own.

Of course, the big question is, did his brain degeneration and aphasia cause the swallowing problem, or did the throat cancer? The physicians say it could be a combination of both illnesses. Does it matter?

All that is important now is keeping Tommy comfortable, peaceful, and pain-free. He is home, in his own bedroom. That's all I can ask for now.

Thirty:
An Untroubled Brow

This is what you look for in a hospice patient: the brow must be untroubled. Smooth, free of lines. There should be no grimacing. The face of the patient must be serene, peaceful.

Tommy has an untroubled brow. His face remains ruddy. His body is calm, arms propped on pillows to keep him comfortable, two pillows behind his sleeping head. A loose sheet covers his quietly breathing, thinning body.

Regularly scheduled doses of morphine and Haldol, with an occasional drop of atropine, are keeping my husband pain-free and tranquil, the goal of hospice.

Tommy is hanging in. "There's no way of telling," doctors and nurses tell me. "Three days, three weeks?" Those estimates are not my husband's concern. His body will leave this earth when it is good and ready. I know this, I am prepared, even though at times I expect Tommy to yawn, raise his arms as if stretching, give me two thumbs up to indicate a good night's sleep, then hop over the bed's steel sides and dress.

That will not happen. My husband, when he decides he has had enough of his blubbering wife, who strokes his head, holds his hand, and whispers, "It's okay if you leave," will slow his breaths and that will be that.

Meanwhile, he is being cared for at home by me and a rotating roster of home health aides, hospice nurses, and CNAs. A few of these people are stellar, like Stuart. Surprise: Stuart is receiving a PhD in nursing before he actually enters nursing school next year. I offered to write to Loyola's administration and tell them Stuart has completed all the necessary coursework.

Others I love—like Rebecca, Qui, and Emile—some I tolerate, and one I insist never steps foot in my house again. Along with inappropriate behavior—e.g., yammering loudly on her cell phone—she texted me constantly from the second floor for various items close at hand. But the final straw was when she decided, without consulting me, to remove all of the supplies I had arranged in rows on our empty queen-size bed and to place them instead on top of dressers, end tables, and windowsills, and on the floor of the shower, hidden by a curtain.

"I wanted the room to look like a bedroom," she explained as she waved her hand atop the empty bedspread.

When the hospice nurse arrived, she shook her head and returned every box of gauze pads; every suction tube, bed pad, pair of disposable underwear, and lotion; and dozens of other supplies back to their original spots. "Much better," she said after all was returned. I hugged her.

I talk to my husband each time I enter the room. Once, I pulled up a chair to read him a letter. Tommy had written it to me in 1996, two years before we married. By the grace of God, I kept it safe. My husband spoke of love, commitment, and promises to care for me—in beautiful handwriting, two pages full. At one point during my reading, he opened his eyes and looked at me, as if to say, *I remember writing that.*

To every visitor who enters the house, I say, "I'd like you to read Tommy's letter." Although his words were meant for me, I fear our friends will recall only the Tommy who struggled with aphasia and could no longer speak, who stopped reading mysteries, or who was unable to fix a broken cabinet door. I want them to know the Tommy who was smart, romantic, and eloquent.

Many loved ones—concerned about my well-being and my ability to pay for round-the-clock nursing care—urged me, upon leaving the hospital, to place Tommy in hospice care in a different setting outside the home. "It will be overwhelming," they predicted.

In a first email update to this group, I admitted, "You were right—it's overwhelming. But I am doing it."

Along with the hired caregivers, I am supported by friends, relatives, and neighbors who visit Tommy and me, who bring food and offer to handle any needed tasks. I have doled out assignments, from picking up Chicago hot dogs to taking my Honda Fit in for servicing.

We will get through this. Meanwhile, we keep watch for an untroubled brow.

Thirty-One:
The Ambivalent Widow

At first, sleeping on Tommy's side of the bed seemed like a good idea: it was a quicker trip to the bathroom and would eliminate the nightly toe stubs I endured during my darkened path from my side.

But in this new space, I hadn't had a full night's sleep since my husband died, on November 2. At first, I blamed it on a sort of post-traumatic stress disorder following three demanding events: my hip replacement surgery, ten days in the hospital with Tommy, and finally an additional twelve at home, with him in hospice care.

Then I dismissed the PTSD theory and fixed on this: Tommy, despite his journey to heaven, wanted his side of the bed back. The 11:00 p.m. and 2:00 a.m. wake-ups I'd been experiencing were really my husband elbowing me over to my side.

So, last night, I obeyed. I returned my iPad to a charger on my bedside table and lined up, on the nearby windowsill, my water bottle, melatonin pills, Tylenol, and Neutrogena hand cream—the same setup prior to my switch. I arranged a mini-memorial on Tommy's bedside table: his portrait, his beloved AM/FM earphones, the forty-year-old wallet he refused to replace, his wristwatch that displayed date along with time, and his wedding band.

Then I scooted onto my side, pulled up the covers, and bawled. My partner was gone. His side of the bed was empty. He would never return for our nightly spooning, or our ritual of him patting me on the tush, me returning a mild pat to his head, and, finally, our exchanging "love yous" before falling asleep.

On my side of the bed, I continued to wail as my stored-up grief filled the room. I realized I'd been so intent on getting my life back together that I hadn't allowed myself to mourn my loss. Oh, I had cried each time I left his thinning and weakening body while he was in hospice, and I had cried when he finally gave up his last breath, but I hadn't cried over his absence.

After I could sob no longer, I turned over, clicked on iTunes, and slept for eight hours. There were bathroom trips cautiously tread, but I willingly took this longer route, and then snuggled into my old spot, hugging his pillow as substitute.

This new role for me as widow has me ambivalent. There are times of dark loneliness and sorrow. But there are also times of relief that my husband's suffering has ended, and there is glaring awareness I have gained new freedom.

Thirty-Two:
Sunday Breakfast, Minus One

It's seven fifteen in the morning, and I'm standing at the kitchen counter, sorting out the bulky Sunday newspaper. "I've got your sports section and the comics," I say out loud. My husband, who died November 2 of this year, is not physically in the room to hear my declaration. But conversing with him eases my raw pain.

After Tommy died, I halted our Sunday routine and stayed away from Dapper's, our usual breakfast place, believing it would be too painful for me to enter without him. But this Sunday, I had to shop at Target in the same mall as the restaurant, so I figured it'd be a good opportunity to test a revisit.

Somehow, I could feel my husband agreeing, celestially pushing for our regular weekend routine. First, though, I had to finish preparing the newspaper that had always accompanied us.

I replicated Tommy's system: Out went the advertising flyers to the recycle bin. Sports and Comics—his first-choice sections—went on top of the pile, followed by News (local and international), Business, Arts, Travel, Real Estate, and Magazine. I took a plastic bag, packed in the specially arranged paper, and drove to Dapper's.

"Can I do this?" I said, as I stood at the entrance's revolving door. Tommy, evidently believing the question was addressed to him, gave me a mystic push and sent me twirling inside.

I stepped to our usual booth. But, since we hadn't been customers for two months because of my hip surgery and my husband's hospitalization and hospice, our place settings weren't arranged. There were no tiny pots of jam, flavored coffee sweeteners, and other items our waitress, Linda, typically set up before our arrival.

"Okay, don't sit there," Linda said, rushing toward me. She grabbed my shoulders and steered me away. I was frozen in the spot, tears staining my eyeglasses. A few of the regulars swiveled to peek but quickly returned to their newspapers and food. Our duo was minus one. My tears and my partner's absence told the story.

As Linda offered alternative booths, I said, "The counter. I want to sit at the counter."

"Perfect," she said.

Linda may have seconded my choice because it could keep her closer to me, perhaps to forestall a second breakdown. But I had another reason: when I first met Tommy, in 1996, he was a regular counter occupant at the Lakeview Diner. Once we became a couple, we moved to a booth.

Now, single, a widow, I decided to honor my husband: I'd become a counter person, too. At this early hour, I was able to spread out. My backpack went to the stool to my right. I unfolded the newspaper atop the bare counter on my left. I was easing in.

In between customers, Linda stood on her side of the counter, elbows up, hands holding her concerned face. I could bawl directly to her without rousing anyone else. "It's so hard being here without him," I said.

"He's here, sweetheart, he's here," she said. "His spirit is here."

"I really felt like he wanted me to be here, and he wanted to come, too."

"Of course," she said.

So I did what I always did, but this time from my new counter seat instead of our old booth: I removed Comics and Sports from the stack I had brought with me. Without worrying about anyone thinking me dotty, I said to my right, "Okay, honey, here are your sections," then placed them on the empty space. As I finished my own parts of the newspaper, I added them to Tommy's pile.

Although his stack never moved, never diminished, I was

okay with the arrangement. I drank my coffee and ate my egg-white Spartan omelet with mozzarella instead of feta, Greek toast, bacon, and fruit. My eyes never left the newspaper.

When I finished my breakfast, Linda brought only one white foam box for leftovers. No need for Tommy's half of waffle, pancake, or cheese omelet.

I placed all of the newspaper sections, including Tommy's stack, back in the plastic bag I had brought from home. I knew I'd never read Comics or Sports, but somehow I couldn't leave them behind.

After I paid the bill, and as I headed for the exit with a light-weight bag of leftovers in one hand and a full bag of newspaper sections in the other, Linda called after me, "See you next week?" Her voice and face were hopeful.

"I'll try," I said. "I'll try."

Then, with Tommy's gentle push, I slowly revolved out the door into my new life.

Thirty-Three:
Ma's Home

If I were clever, I would've recorded Tommy's voice declaring, "Ma's home!" and then jerry-rigged the machine to start as soon as the front door opened. If I had done that, my homecoming might have been easier. As it was, following a return flight from Boston, when I placed my carry-on in the front hall, I was greeted by silence.

While Tommy's death was sudden and unexpected, my caregiving for him was long and challenging. He was diagnosed with FTD/PPA in 2009, but there were signs my husband had the illness years before.

As Tommy's symptoms worsened, he relinquished his car keys and I became his chauffeur. I feared letting him venture out alone, or even allowing him to being in the house on his own. Trips to my out-of-town daughters ceased, because he would not be able to call 911 if he got into trouble. My calendar revolved around him. On Tuesdays, if his golfing buddies had a game and took responsibility for him, I was free to make plans with friends. When the boys bailed, I'd take Tommy to practice golf, and then we'd lunch together. I did not want him to be alone, to be without company.

Now, with my husband gone and my job as caregiver canceled, I've booked tickets to Boston in November and Los Angeles in December. I've made lunch plans on days of the week that aren't Tuesday. I take my time returning in the morning from the health club, unlike in the past, when I made sure to get back before Tommy woke.

Tommy and I would have celebrated our fifteenth wedding anniversary on January 13, 2013—an occasion we looked forward to. We planned to grow old together. We were content and happy. We rarely argued—we were satisfied sitting on our facing couches, watching our favorite television shows, and, early on, taking turns with the crossword puzzle.

My new solo routine is this: before I go to my side of the bed, where I evidently belong, I pause at Tommy's picture. I bring my fingers to my lips and then place them on his photographed face. "Love you," I say. I hear his response, clear as day: "Love you, too!"

Then I imagine my husband giving me another pat on my tush, this one indicating, *You go, girl. It's your time now.*

Thirty-Four:
The Takeover

The first thing I tackled were the hundreds of black plastic take-home containers and their sibling clear plastic lids that were jumbled on kitchen cupboard shelves. How had we accumulated so many? Why were they in such a hodgepodge? And, more important, how had I let this mess get out of hand? I was the cook, Tommy handled cleanup and storage, but that was no excuse for this mortifying clutter.

With my husband gone over a month, I felt ready to start clearing out many of the piles that had stacked up over time. The mountains of containers that threatened an avalanche whenever I opened the cabinet door were just one example of my indifference.

"My fault," I admitted. I was conversing with Tommy because I felt guilty about the expunging about to take place. "I neglected too many things," I said, not expecting a response. "I didn't pay attention to what was sprouting in corners, on shelves, in drawers."

This cleansing, and more that was to occur that day, was part of an effort to take back my house. Without realizing it, I had ceded it to my husband. Not just the exterior, where he had tended the garden, painted the front porch and stairs, and stained the back deck, but it appeared I had turned over the interior space as well.

After the cupboard was tidy, I started on the coat closet. I planned to donate Tommy's wardrobe to Goodwill, believing the absence would ease my journey. But I paused at the first hanger. "Not your high school jacket," I said. "We'll keep that."

Dark green wool, with gray leather sleeves, STEINMETZ H.S. bannered on the back, '53 on one sleeve, and TOM on the front, the jacket was not an original—it was retro, but exactly like the one my young student would have worn in his senior year.

"And not the fedora," I said, as I stood on a step stool to reach the top closet shelf for the dozens of baseball caps and hats he had collected. "Yeah, you were a hunk when you wore your black leather jacket and topped it with that fedora." I pictured him, arms akimbo, giving a shake to show off.

After filling one large bag with items that I could part with, I moved to the second floor. In my takeover plan, I was not only decluttering but also trading places. I coveted Tommy's bathroom, which was within our master bedroom and had a shower stall, unlike the tub with showerhead in my bathroom that had me clinging to grab bars for dear life.

Now in Tommy's former bathroom, I pressed open the three-mirrored doors that shielded his medicine cabinet. I tossed out hardened tubes of sunblock, congealed shaving cream, fossilized hair tonic, and prescription medications.

With a soapy rag, I whisked each shelf clean. I studied the mirror to be sure no apparition glowered back. Clear, so I made trip after trip from my former bathroom to my new master bath. Cosmetics, Q-tips, cotton pads, women's deodorant—I lined them all up on the two lower shelves I could reach without a step stool.

Next, it was time to clear out rows and shelves of blue jeans, shorts, shoes, slacks, and sweaters that were spread throughout two closets. Again, I hesitated. I could not give to Goodwill the sport coat and suit I insisted my betrothed buy for our Las Vegas wedding weekend in 1998. My frugal fiancé protested he'd never wear those fancy duds again, and he was partially right: the sport coat had perhaps a yearly airing, but the suit hung abandoned in the closet for the remainder of our marriage.

I would not toss out his painter's outfit, either: labor-ripped long and short blue jeans, a red sweatshirt and orange T-shirt, and a crimson Harvard baseball cap—all speckled with the blue of our porch. The set would remain here on a hook, just as he had left it, all reminding me of Tommy's tender maintenance of our home before his cruel illness interfered.

The long row of T-shirts and sweatshirts my husband bought at resale shops slowed me down, too. I decided to keep them all and use them as sleepwear.

When I descended to the basement, I was confronted by several golf bags and clubs, dozens of boxes of Caldwell balls, paintbrushes and opened buckets of blue paint. Instead of sorting them for donation, I turned and retreated upstairs. "Not today," I said. "Not today."

Thirty-Five:
The Opposite of Caregiving

The peace lily (*Spathiphyllum*) features dark green foliage and a large white flower. It is a strictly indoor plant that takes medium light, blooms year-round, and is very forgiving. That is, until the unlucky houseplant met me.

"Sarah," I led off in my email, "will you take Tommy's plants?" My neighbor had admired them on a previous visit. I watched, guilt shadowing my face, as she lifted a watering can from its dusty shelf and approached the peace lily.

Tenderly, as I had seen my husband do, she watered the plant, along with all of the others he had cared for over the years. The drooping leaves appeared to heave a sigh of relief, soon brightening and popping up as the water I had thoughtlessly denied them quenched their thirst.

My gift to my neighbor of the half dozen houseplants was part of my effort to divest myself of anything that required my care and attention. I had spent a good part of my second marriage taking care of my husband—willingly and faithfully—and now, with his passing, I wanted to be free of responsibility.

It wasn't only houseplants I was rejecting, but also pets. "No, no dogs," I'd reply to those who suggested a furry companion to assuage my typical widow loneliness. "A cat?" they'd pose. "Much easier to care for. No walking in the winter. Just a litter box."

I'd turn down that idea, too. "Expensive," I'd respond. We had spent a fortune over the years in veterinary bills for Sasha, who died at nine, and Buddy, who lived to fourteen. While we loved our golden retrievers like children, the financial cost was, in truth, only one factor; the responsibility and, more important, the pain of animals' eventual loss also made me resistant to the suggestion.

And, there'd be the memories a new pet would bring. "Like clockwork," a neighbor reminded me. "You, Tommy, and Buddy, walking around the park at six in the morning. Then there'd be Tommy shouting at Buddy, 'No, no, no,' as the dog headed for a mud puddle. And before Tommy could change Buddy's direction, there'd be your dog, plopping like a hippo."

I laughed as I recalled that repeated scene. No, no more dogs. No more images of my husband racing to catch up with our golden. No more reminders of my glee as I watched Tommy fetch Buddy from his makeshift pond. "I'll hose him off in the basement," he'd say, more amused than angry.

"A roommate—that's what you need," suggested my daughters. "You've got two spare bedrooms in your big house, you've admitted to loneliness in the afternoons—get a roommate for company and extra cash."

It was true the two spaces I had reserved for my out-of-town daughters and their families have gone mostly unused, expect for brief visits twice a year. I thought about their idea. Thought about the money that could help me pay bills. Thought about taking in a young student or actor, or even an airline pilot who would welcome our proximity to O'Hare. I even started composing an ad for that last possibility.

But then I got depressed. I had images of lowering the volume on my TV so I wouldn't disturb my housemates. My 4:00 a.m. MSNBC show that accompanies my early rising might have to be curtailed out of concern for the stranger needing his or her sleep down the hall.

I saw myself opening doors to find clothing tossed on the floor, unmade beds, which paying renters would have every right to leave. I imagined myself morphing into Mother, waving away their objections and insisting they eat a little something before their class, performance, or flight.

"Go, leave the laundry," I heard myself saying. "You'll be late. I'll take care of it."

Then, despite my best intentions, I couldn't doubt the vision of me lying awake, listening for a late-night key in the door, just as I once did with my flesh and blood.

"No, no boarders," I told them.

"But your loneliness," my daughters reminded me.

"There's nothing wrong with being temporarily lonely," I said. "Right now, I really don't want to talk to anyone. I want to sit on the couch and eat my meals while watching TV."

Of course, I know a time will come when lack of responsibility moves from respite to emptiness, when I will long for a beating heart nearby. Until then, I will talk to myself and to my departed husband. For a smidgen of caretaking, I'll tend to the mixed bouquet on my kitchen table. Trim stems, change water, add crystal. I think I can handle that.

Thirty-Six:
The Handyman

"We'll have to scrape off the old paint," the handyman says. "Won't look good if we just put another layer on top of the old."

He looks up at me, likely wishing there was a man of the house who would better understand his diagnosis. I doubt he appreciates this woman who seems to be counting dollars as he talks.

Yes, I'm counting costs, but my faraway look is also linked to memories on this porch. I see me sitting on the top stair, my golden retriever Buddy tucked tight next to me. I see Tommy rounding the corner on his Schwinn. The dog barks in joy; I smile with relief that my impaired husband has made it home safely.

Once the handyman has finished inspecting the front porch, I'll lead him to the back deck, which will need new staining. Nothing to strip here, just another layer to bring the wood back to a healthy shine. Again, images will interfere with his chatter. The glass-topped table is now stored in the basement, along with the wrapped umbrella. Four chairs with rattan arms peeling off and rain-stained seat cushions are the table's companions.

When Tommy was healthy, we'd host pre–Labor Day parties year after year. Some sixty friends and neighbors would claim spots at the outdoor table, or at the green bench in the yard, or scatter themselves in the kitchen. "No, no more parties," I told guests who were wondering at the absence of email invitations this year. Already privy to Tommy's aphasia, which made him unable to join in on conversations and enjoy social situations, they didn't ask for explanations.

The basement floor is the last area that needs the handyman's review and estimate. The space still holds a treadmill, but the workman's bench my husband used in the early days of our twelve years here is cleared of all tools. Two golf bags have already been donated to Goodwill, and I will gift the scores of balls Tommy couldn't resist buying.

Against all advice typically doled out to recent widows— such as don't make a major move for a year following a spouse's death—I have already decided to sell our house. There are rational reasons: A three-bedroom home is too large for just me. There is no longer a dog, so the fenced-in backyard and proximity to the park are not necessities. There is no gardener husband, so the vegetable plots that only he tended will lie fallow. The upkeep is more than my limited budget can handle.

While some may think my reasoning is limp and I am rushing into things, in truth, this decision has been simmering for several years. "When Tommy can't take care of the house any longer," I'd tell loved ones who worried over the burden, "we'll consider a move to an apartment."

At times, I'd pose the idea to my husband: "Wouldn't it be lovely to be in a high-rise overlooking the lake, with someone else handling upkeep?"

"Feet-first," Tommy would reply, confirming his desire never to move from this house.

So, without his vote, I'm eyeing one-bedroom rentals in downtown Chicago, with maintenance included in the rent. My new home should have a doorman and a balcony, and a washer and drier in the unit; be near public transportation, so I can turn in my costly leased car; and be walking distance to attractions. A health club in the building and an outdoor pool would be lovely, too.

While the handyman does his part in prepping the house for a spring sale, I will go through closets, shelves, and files and decide what must be transported to a very downsized apartment. I will continue donating Tommy's clothing and sporting equipment to Goodwill. On Wednesday mornings, before the trash trucks arrive, I'll dump clutter and old files into the bins at the curb.

When the realtor brings prospective buyers to my house, I will leave the premises. While I'd be happy to see a young family as the new owners, with children occupying the bedrooms, with a dog who frolics in the yard, with a handyman husband who'll fill the workbench with new tools, I'd rather not be in earshot.

Moving forward, independent—that's where my thoughts must travel now. New year, new chapter, with Tommy's spirit as my dear roommate. I'm sure he'll adjust.

Thirty-Seven:
Like Mother, Like Daughter. Or Not.

I'm cooking the ground beef, pressing it flat, turning it over, and stirring until it darkens. The meat is an ingredient in a recipe for Italian-style sloppy joes that I clipped from the newspaper.

As I watch the meat brown, I think of my mother, who with her famous chili mac performed a similar coloration during my childhood. As she enters my brain, I imagine her smiling at the sight of her daughter cooking. This is an unfamiliar activity for me. Simple tabletop grilling, microwaving, ordering out, or carrying out was my usual pattern.

But something changed after my husband died. Without the care and worry that absorbed me, I now have extra hours in the day. And since my menu is no longer focused on the vegetarian dishes he preferred, I have a taste for home-cooked meals with meat or chicken.

I'm not a creative cook who tosses in a pinch of this or a handful of that; I'm a recipe follower who uses sauce-stained fingertips to trace each ingredient and step. I haven't opted for fancy cookware, save for the cast-iron pot one of my daughters insisted I add. But for tonight's dish, I'm using my weathered frying pan.

My mother, back in her kitchen in the three-room apartment we lived in above our store, used an electric frying pan for her cuisine—as aged and well worn as my current cordless. I can still see her, attired in a Swirl apron, wearing the wedge slippers she changed into from her preferred high heels.

As I thought about Mom and the commonality of our cooking, another notion plopped in my head: we both bear the title of widow. In her case, she was very young, just forty-five years old, when she got the label, while I am nearly three decades older.

My father died in 1958, at forty-eight. He was a three-pack-a-day unfiltered-Camel smoker, was overweight, and had diabetes, so his demise from a heart attack was not a shock but rather a fear that darkened my childhood.

My husband died November 2, 2012, at age seventy-seven, from throat cancer. "Was he a smoker?" doctors asked. I knew Tommy was a heavy smoker before we met, perhaps on a level similar to Dad's overindulgence. But I understood he had quit cold turkey at about fifty.

As I continued the recipe, stirring the browned meat into the already softened onions, then adding red wine, canned tomatoes, tomato paste, oregano, red pepper flakes, and salt, I remembered Mom's words after she became a widow: "I never want to be a burden to my kids."

This pledge pushed her to try to learn how to drive. She enlisted her brother, my uncle Hy, to pick her up on Saturdays for lessons on quiet streets. But after just a few outings, she returned to the apartment she and I shared, tears in her blue eyes. "I give up," I remember her saying as she sank into the couch.

Poor Mom believed it was too late for her to take the wheel, so she accepted the proposal of a man twenty years her senior who could put her in the passenger seat. (This turned out to be a lousy marriage that required her to clip coupons. Her husband declined with Alzheimer's but still outlived my mom—who died at sixty-seven—for many years.)

This is where Mother and I part ways. I was fortunate to enjoy a happy second marriage, free of contention or serious belt tightening. Tommy was only three years my senior, and I was the one who insisted he learn how to drive. While he also suffered from a deteriorating brain disease, he left this earth with me still strolling on it.

Secondly, unlike my mother, I'd never consider myself a burden to my kids; a sometimes embarrassment, a frequent meddler, an expert at passive-aggressive behavior, but a burden? Never.

Not only can I operate a vehicle (even manual, if need be), but I manage my own business and can program a DVR, set up Apple devices, and build a blog.

While Mom would likely be proud of these accomplishments, in my heart of hearts I know it's the recent cooking that brings a smile to her ethereal face. In our years together, I never asked her to teach me how to cook, or do the handicrafts she was skilled at, like knitting, needlepoint, and crocheting. I wonder now, was that hurtful to her?

Odd that cooking has become a new hobby, drawing my mother back into my consciousness. Perhaps her spirit sees a window of opportunity. She's successfully led me to the stove—could a ball of yarn be next?

Thirty-Eight:
Odd Number

There were five of us seated around the table—circular, so much better than rectangular, where an empty chair would've been haunting. Four dear friends who didn't want me alone on my aborted fifteen-year wedding anniversary treated me to dinner at a favorite neighborhood restaurant. It was the same spot Tommy and I, and this very same group, celebrated at each year.

"So sweet," my daughters said when they heard of our friends' kind gesture. "Should we pick up the check, like we've done before?"

"No," I said. "Not this time."

I remembered our grateful surprise at anniversary dinners the previous years. "Your meals are covered," the waiter said as he cleared the table. "Your daughters paid for it."

"Another round of drinks!" my friends joked. I and my husband, a stepfather to my generous girls, grasped hands and smiled. Misty eyes for both of us.

What was Tommy thinking? I wondered back then. Did he consider how much our lives had changed since our marriage all those years ago? I know that's where my thoughts flew. He still had a bit of a vocabulary at dinner 2011, but occasionally one of our friends turned to me with a blank look, hoping I could interpret my husband's patchwork language.

By the time the six of us celebrated on January 13, 2012, Tommy's greedy aphasia had stolen all speech. My heart sank as he sat quietly while the rest of us debated our usual topics.

This year, 2013, I was the odd number at the table. I had been a widow for only just over two months, so the feeling of being a "third wheel" hadn't yet entered my brain. But I remember how it nagged after my divorce from my first husband.

Initially, when he left our thirty-year marriage, which was often unhappy, I felt like a kid let out of school. I ate pizza on the couch, filled the house with overnight guests who often stayed for months, and hosted dinners that squeezed our dining room.

But after four years of this freedom, loneliness crept in. I missed being married. I wanted to be part of a couple again. I hated being the gal left at the wedding or bar mitzvah guarding the purses while couples danced.

I put an ad in the *Chicago Reader* (the pre–online match-making option), attended a few singles events, told my friends I wanted to be fixed up, and went on a series of dates that either ended the same evening or continued for several months.

And while none of these swains turned out to be "the one," I did enjoy primping for an evening out and feeling like half a pair.

In the end, Tommy and I met through neither of the methods listed above but instead, as the song suggests, "on the street where we lived." After our first date—I asked him out—we became a couple. We each found what we wanted in a partner, and married within two years.

Although his friends say he fell head over heels when he met me, I think Tommy was a more content single than I was. His first marriage wasn't nearly as long as mine, and there were no children, so there appeared to be nothing he longed for or missed.

Unless it was someone to cherish, because that's what my husband did from first date to last breath. As I've been rifling through dresser drawers in preparation for an eventual sale of our home, I've found stacks of yellow-lined notes bundled in rubber bands, each bearing a sentiment from a love-struck middle-aged man who paused every day to let me know he felt as if he had won the lottery.

As for me, I reveled in being cherished by someone I loved. But just as much, I was thrilled to be part of a couple again, to be a married woman. When Tommy introduced me to his longtime friends, and when we double-dated with mine, all my third-wheel feelings dissolved.

This time around, I'm not sure how long it will take for that sense of being the odd number to hit. Truthfully, I'm hoping it stays away for quite a while. I'd rather savor the specialness I felt in my second marriage, where two was the perfect number.

Thirty-Nine:
Growing Stronger

"Please don't load them too heavy," I said to the Trader Joe's cashier as he unfolded and stretched out a few brown grocery bags. "I have to carry them into the house myself."

Kevin turned to me, first with a questioning look and then with one of recognition. He had learned through the store's grapevine that my husband had died in November.

"No problem," he said, and then pulled out several more bags to spread my purchases among the collection building on the counter.

Like all of the other members of the TJ's staff, Kevin had witnessed the ritual that Tommy and I performed every Sunday morning at eight o'clock until my husband's hospitalization. It started like this: After we parked our car in the lot, which was still not filled at that early hour, Tommy would head for the shopping-cart corral and extract two. He'd hand me mine first, and then we'd meet up inside at the floral display,

"Your assignment, if you wish to accept it," I'd joke, "is soy milk, bananas, strawberries, and orange juice."

With that directive, Tommy would push his cart toward the bakery goods.

Sticky pecan buns were not on the list of needs I recorded in the reporter's notebook I keep on our kitchen counter. Neither was apple pie. But my husband regularly added one or the other pastry to his cart. These were his freebies, and I think he enjoyed this bit of independence from his wife's rigid list.

Tommy would then depart, picking up the items I had requested. After a few minutes, he'd return to find me and get his next assignment.

"Good," I'd say as I scanned his cart and checked off "milk," "ban," "straw," "OJ" from my list. Then I'd instruct him, "Pickles, marinated mushrooms, stuffed green olives, applesauce."

Tommy and I would repeat this back-and-forth until we finished my list. With his mission completed, he'd head off, leaving me with his cart and bounty. Solo, I'd push mine and drag his behind me, like a mother with one cooperative and one unruly child.

I'd head to a checkout counter manned by a familiar face. If it were a regular like Kevin, I wouldn't have to give this spiel: "Consider these two carts as one. Pretend there is no bar between them. One order. One bill."

I'd feel it helpful to add a backstory: "We used to shop with one cart," I'd say. "But then I'd find myself with my arms overloaded as I tried to catch up with my husband. This is easier."

"Got it," the neophyte would claim, but then he would total up the first cart, slap his forehead, and say, "Oh, sorry, force of habit." So you can see why we so appreciated Kevin and his like.

As purchases from the twin carts were being bagged, I'd start to seek a visual. Tommy had a habit, once he relinquished his cart, of wandering the aisles. Another bit of independence, I'm sure.

If I were in a bratty mood, I'd wheel out the condensed and paid-for cart to the Honda—my version of revenge for his disappearance. "Send him out when he shows up," I'd tell Kevin. "Will do," he'd say. I never knew if Kevin had picked up on Tommy's condition or if he figured he was just another impatient spouse who had better things to do than wait for grocery bags to be filled.

I wouldn't pull that shtick very often, as I didn't want to cause Tommy one bit of anxiety. As for him, he never seemed perturbed by my leave-taking. He'd soon catch up with me at the opened trunk and watch a bit as I struggled with the first shopping bag. Then he'd grin and nudge me aside to complete the loading.

On the day I was doing my solitary shopping—not a Sunday,

because it was still too painful to visit the store on our day—Kevin hoisted one of the filled bags in the air, then handed it to me. "What do you think?" he asked.

I lifted it up, testing its weight to decide if I'd be able to transfer first from cart to trunk, then from trunk up the back stairs to the kitchen.

"I think I can manage," I said.

At home, the extra bags and the absence of a muscled helper required several trips from car to kitchen. *Cardio,* I told myself. *Building muscle. Growing stronger.*

Then I imagined Tommy in his celestial abode, grinning. Not from my struggle, though, but from pride. "Knew you could do it," he'd say, as he raised his hands to give me two thumbs up.

Forty:
Without a Trace

"It might be best if you stash some of the family pictures," the realtor says. "People coming through want a clean landscape, no traces of the current owner."

I realize he's trying to be gentle, for he's aware of the circumstances that led to my putting my house on the market. I'm not offended by his suggestion. We're a team with the same goal: sell my three-bedroom house, which has become too large and too lonely without my husband. If we're successful, then we'll move me into a rental apartment that will better suit my budget and solo life.

"I guess I could declutter," I say. My gaze travels around the rooms on the first floor. The dining room table holds a framed photograph of Tommy on his Schwinn. I love that picture because it's a testimony to his amazing spirit. Despite my husband's challenges, he hopped on his bike every afternoon while I stood watch at the window and paced until he returned.

I hit pause on my reverie and promise the realtor, "I'll handle it before the showing."

"Take your time," he says, and puts a hand on my shoulder that tells me he sympathizes.

When he leaves, I move to our upright piano, its top decorated with photos of the two golden retrievers who gave us so many years of sweet companionship. Where to hide these temporarily? The piano bench! I open the lid and place the three pictures on the Rogers and Hart songbook.

The second floor is the real challenge, for it's not only Tommy and the dogs hogging every surface and shelf, but daughters, grandchildren, and my brother and his family—all smiling back at me with memories of our younger, innocent, hopeful selves.

I slow my task because each photo must be studied. Their backstories flash in front of me, like the crawl at the bottom of a TV screen. Instead of sports scores or weather advisories, the line that enters my vision reminds me: *This one must've been taken sixteen years ago, because my oldest grandson is just a baby here.* My daughters and their partners, Tommy and I, and Sasha, the first of our dogs, are sprawled across our queen-size bed.

Everyone in the scene gleams. The joy of a new grandchild and the feeling of family togetherness are palpable. Now that I think of it, I believe some of Tommy's happiness in that photo was due to this new family he had won.

Without a piano bench to use as storage, I find a carton to hold the second floor's larger collection. I lift a photo from a bookshelf. It displays my husband and me and my brother and sister-in-law. We are at some party that I can't recall, but it must've been special, because the men are in sport jackets and the women in fancy clothing. "Is anything wrong with Tommy?" is the line that this photo generates. "He seems to be repeating things."

"It's not Alzheimer's," I tell my brother. "He forgot to take his thyroid meds for several weeks, and he's a bit muddled." Wishful thinking, I realize now. Not Alzheimer's, but the first evidence of brain degeneration as miserable as the better-known illness.

There are wedding photos everywhere. Tommy and I posing as newlyweds, smiles nearly as bright as the Las Vegas lights in the hotel we picked for our venue. Here's a crowd photo of my daughters, their partners, my grandson, my brother and sister-in-law, and friends who could fly in for our January 13, 1998, wedding. I gather all of these testaments to our happy union and open a dresser drawer to tuck them into.

On the nightstand next to our bed, the makeshift altar I created to honor Tommy after he died is still intact. One by one, I place each totem in a drawer. But once strangers traverse my clean landscape, I'll retrieve and return his beloved possessions to their rightful spot.

When I am finished de-cluttering and my home no longer bears traces of my old life, I head out the door. The realtor is due soon with a prospect. I hope they have children, a dog, and, please, a camera.

Forty-One:
The Sign

The sign is actually quite simple—just the realtor's name, his company's name, and his contact information. It stands to the right of the stairs that lead up to the front porch. Because it's a windy day, the sign sways, but the post that anchors it remains steady.

The sign must've been planted when I was elsewhere in the house, because this is my first sighting. From my window view, I see that the message is printed on both sides. *Good idea*, I think. *That way, passersby coming from either direction can learn that our house is up for sale.*

I say "*our* house" because I can't yet bring myself to omit my husband from its ownership. And perhaps that's one reason I hesitated in allowing the sign to be erected in the first place.

"Can we put it on the market without a sign?" I asked my realtor.

"If that's what you want, that's fine," he said.

"I'm just not ready."

"No problem."

I'm not sure why I balked. After all, my neighbors had followed my life and Tommy's illness with steady concern and support, and all were aware of my decision. "We hate to see you go," they said, "but we understand."

When we bought the house in 2000, these neighbors came to our door bearing a flowering plant and a plate of cookies.

"Welcome," they said, and then handed me a flyer for a block party that was scheduled later that month.

One by one, I met nearly everyone on our street. I've been witness to pregnant bellies and adoptions that brought forth children whom I've watched sprout taller every year. And I've seen puppies grow from wild frolickers to snoozers on front lawns.

The block parties continue as annual events and each year spread farther up and down the closed-off street as new young families discover us. "We've blossomed into a small-town square, straight out of Norman Rockwell" is how I described our last party.

Perhaps Tommy's and my entry into the neighborhood all those years ago was made easier because of our own golden retriever, for this is a dog-addicted neighborhood. There's a park at the end of our block that attracts early risers who meet daily to release their pets to delirious chasing of tennis balls, and one another.

After our dog died in June of 2012, at the age of fourteen, I'd still return to the park in the morning light and imagine Buddy in the mix. He was just one and a half years old when we chose him from a shelter. For a few weeks after he was gone, I'd return to the park with my jacket pockets still filled with treats, a tennis ball, and a plastic bag. I'd sit on a bench and chat with friends while watching the dogs play. Eventually, though, I deposited half a dozen balls on one neighbor's porch and boxes of treats on another's.

As I think of it, perhaps I didn't want to put up the For Sale sign because I thought it would break Tommy's heart, even if he might be too remote to notice. "Feet-first," he'd say whenever anyone asked if we'd ever leave.

Lately, though, I believe my husband would approve of my decision to sell and move to a rental apartment. He knows I'm useless with a hammer, am terrified of a power mower, and need more than a stepladder to change a lightbulb. These were his tasks, and I'm certain he'd rather I keep my hands off them.

Because of the way he cared for me during our seventeen years together, I don't think Tommy's keen on my living here alone, despite the safety of our neighborhood. In fact, as I do the nightly security check—lock windows and doors, turn on outside lights, and draw drapes—I can sense him in my shadow, double-checking my work.

I realize that in the morning, when I do the reverse of the nighttime check—open the drapes, turn off the porch lights, and unlock the front door to retrieve the newspapers—the first thing I'll spot is the sign. Perhaps I should brace myself for the expected pang.

But it could be that after a night's sleep, I'll see it in a different light—not as a prompt of old memories, but as a guidepost to my new chapter.

Forty-Two:
Un-couching the Potato

After I hit the SUBMIT button, I felt as proud as if I had just earned a degree. My accomplishment certainly couldn't compare to matriculating, but for me, promising—via a paid-for ticket—to go out to an evening event was nearly as daunting.

It all started with a demand from one of my longtime friends. "Now that Tommy is gone," she said, "you've got to get off your couch and go out in the evenings." She is a persuasive woman, someone who easily wins any debate.

She pressed on: "I remember you used to love going to plays."

"I have to go to bed at eight so I can get up at four and start my work," I said.

I assumed she'd applaud my entrepreneurial spirit, but instead she countered, "That's nuts." I have heard that diagnosis from many others.

I once could use my husband as an excuse for staying in. There was a time when he and I were frequent theatergoers, and there were many evenings when we joined friends for dinner. But as his brain degeneration worsened and his aphasia left him unable to speak one word, we discarded those pastimes.

"It just wasn't fun anymore," I told her. She's a very empathetic person, so I thought this tack might get her to go easy on me. "Tommy couldn't join in on conversations at a restaurant," I continued, "and at the theater, I'd worry if he went to the men's room on his own. He refused to let me stand outside the door, but I was afraid he wouldn't be able to find his way back to our seats."

My poignant story did slow her down, but it was temporary. "So, now?" she asked.

"I love TV," I admitted. "For me, a perfect evening is bringing a dinner tray to the couch and watching one of the shows I taped the night before." I felt my heart lighten as I conjured the scene: bliss for me, but evidently a horror story for my friend, who was wrinkling her nose as if my laptop meal had gone sour.

"That's awful," she said.

I ignored her disdain and for a moment continued my meditation. Except for the dinner tray, that was how my husband and I spent our evenings. We stretched out on couches that faced each other, and instead of chatting across the coffee table, we focused on a procedural drama, such as the entire *Law & Order* franchise, that was playing out on the screen.

Amazingly, for two people so different from each other, we enjoyed the very same television shows and routine. No disputes came from our dual couches; we simply scrolled through "My Recordings" to decide on the one we'd watch for the evening.

"That's why our marriage has lasted as long as it has," I often told friends. We were nearing our fifteen-year anniversary, which I considered a record for the second time around and for such a mismatched pair. I'd further explain, "Tommy's Gentile; I'm Jewish. He has no kids; I've got two and grandchildren. I have a master's degree; Tommy never went to college. He lived on a budget; I was married to a doctor. But we both love staying home and watching the same television programs."

In fact, our passion for our couch-potato lifestyle was so strong that we came to begrudge invitations for evenings out. "We're hosting Passover dinner," another very longtime friend had said, "but I know you don't want to come." Sweetly, the invitations continued, despite her anticipating my response.

But now, with Tommy gone, without my head wrapped around his caregiving, my nights on the couch are starting to fray. I'm getting lonely. I admit that evenings out to the theater, to dinner, to the event I just ordered tickets for, are becoming more appealing.

I'm even managing my dislike for nighttime driving by using taxicabs. And I'm adjusting to getting gussied up as the sky darkens. To prevent head and eye droops as the evening wears on, I take catnaps. Slowly, one event at a time, one limb at a time, I'm peeling this small and stubborn body off the couch.

Forty-Three:
Carless in Chicago

I am in a window seat on the CTA Red Line traveling toward Howard. When I reach that stop, I will transfer to the Purple Line, which will take me to Main. From there, I will walk about six short blocks to my friend Ruth's house.

As I look out the window at the high-rise buildings and landscapes skimming by, I contemplate my new role as someone without a car. I do not feel deprived. In fact, I am enjoying a new sense of calm, relief.

Being carless is a fresh experience for me, for I have been a licensed driver since the age of sixteen. With learner's permit in hand, I had my first lesson with my dad. I don't remember the exact details, but I can easily see me in the driver's seat of his Buick, propped up on at least two cushions to have a view over the steering wheel. My dad, Irving, is in the passenger's seat. A Camel he is smoking is dropping ashes on his shirt, but he is unperturbed. He brushes them to the car's floor with his left hand, while his right maintains steady drags on the cigarette.

"You're going too slow!" he is shouting at me. I am cautious, because Dad was the opposite. I had no intention of emulating his speed, or his habit of weaving in and out of cars like a NASCAR competitor.

We both survived those early lessons, and I emerged with his perfect method for parallel parking. It is a skill I taught my daughters, my recently deceased husband, and my grandson.

I'm enjoying this musing as an El train passenger. "It's my meditation," I told my daughter after the first of my carless trips. She worries about my anxiety level, certain it will topple me one day. "I study the view, the people entering and exiting. I eavesdrop on conversations. I can feel my blood pressure dropping."

"Okay," she says, mollified for the moment. My child is worried that I gave up my Honda Fit hastily.

"Couldn't you have held on to it until you moved downtown?" she asked. "Why now, when you're still in your house?"

I knew my explanation would just reinforce her picture of me sizzling like someone receiving electroshock therapy. But I gave it a shot: "I had an entire year left on my car lease," I said. "If I couldn't return it to a dealer, I'd owe $3,000. The only way to get a manager to accept it was to be sure it was in perfect condition."

I revealed how my rides in the Fit had turned into episodes of angst. I was terrified backing out of supermarket lots, certain I would ding a fender. I was sure my bumper would become a victim at a yellow light when I stopped and the cabbie behind me didn't.

"Okay, I understand that," she said. "But what about grocery shopping? I don't see you schlepping paper bags on the bus."

"Peapod home delivery!" I said. "They shop at Mariano's, the produce and groceries are terrific, they carry the Intelligentsia coffee I love, and they even have the alstroemeria flowers I've been using to perk up the house for showings."

"Sounds like you've got it covered, Mom."

"Just think of it," I went on. "I'm reducing my expenses, getting exercise by walking stairs to the platform, and protecting the environment." As I recited these benefits, I was heroic, altruistic, deserving of a medal.

"Good for you, Mom," she said.

My reflection of this mother-daughter conversation was coming to an end as I alighted from the Purple Line at my Evanston stop and walked to Ruth's house.

"You made it," my friend said, as she stood at her open door. She led me in and waited as I unzipped my boots and removed each layer of my wardrobe.

"No problem," I said, dropping into the nearest armchair. "Water, please."

Ruth looked at me and, from her seat on a facing couch, said, "Marshall will drive you home later."

I'm certain I would've rallied and successfully tiptoed the treacherous icy blocks to the Purple Line stop. And, heavily layered, I could have handled waiting on the windy platform for the Red Line. Knowing me, after carefully descending the slippery steps at Sheridan, I would've been fine sharing seats or aisles with bulky-coated rush-hour passengers. But I didn't want to be rude.

"If you insist," I said.

Forty-Four:
Chatterbox

"You go here, and you go here." I am talking to my laundry.

At my feet are two baskets. As I draw clothing from the laundry chute, where it has landed after being tossed down from the second floor, I alert my blue jeans that they are being dropped into "colors," and Tommy's undershirts—which I have taken as my own—are learning they are joining "whites."

Four months after my husband's death, I find myself talking out loud. Not only in the privacy of my house, where there's no one around to declare me loony, but also on the street. Listen to this recent conversation: "Good girl! That was clever to keep the Walgreens receipt so you could exchange the blue nail polish that was crap."

Fortunately, passersby assumed I had a Bluetooth stuck in my ear and that there was someone else on the other side of the wireless. Naw, it was just me, enjoying the sound of my voice.

There are several reasons I've become a chatterbox in my rookie widow state: first, because I work out of my home, and there is no longer a dog or a husband to benefit from my cooing, instructions, or revelations, I could possibly go an entire day without speaking. I doubt that's good for my vocal cords or mental health.

When Tommy was alive, I was a big talker. When he lost his ability to speak, we often communicated through simulations of the parlor game Charade.

If I couldn't figure out what he was trying to tell me, I'd do my shtick: "Are you asking me a question? Are you telling me something? Does it have to do with a television show? A woman? A man?" And so on. Sometimes our back-and-forth took quite a bit of time. But I refused to give up until I got the correct answer. And when I did, I'd give my spouse a happy kiss. Perhaps it should've been Tommy bussing me, but I always believed he deserved the reward because of his spirited efforts.

Even though my husband couldn't hold a conversation, that didn't stop me from talking to him. He could understand everything I said, and had no problem with memory, so I made sure to keep him in the loop of my daily trivialities.

"You'll never believe what happened today," I might say. And then I'd relate some stupid story that was likely boring, but he was game to behave as if it were absorbing. If the tale made me a winner, Tommy would smile and give me thumbs up. But if it was my folly I was confessing, he'd shake his head and return to the TV. Either reaction satisfied me.

After he died, there was no need to keep up the chatter, since he wasn't around to hear it. So I kept quiet. And eventually, the absence of voice overwhelmed the house. It sank into the curtains, was absorbed in the carpet, leeched onto the walls.

That's when I started talking. Not only to myself, but also to inanimate objects. "Good morning, Herman," I'll say to the stone hippo Tommy bought at a crafts show. It's a heavy and odd piece of art, but my husband liked it. It sits on a bathroom sill and gets a stroke on its smooth surface along with my words.

Not only *objets d'art* are privy to my babble, but so are the aforementioned laundry, a teapot, my iMac, various stuffed animals, and bouquets of flowers—and I have been known to thank a jug of milk for not spoiling on its sell-by date. There are also the well-known questions you may share but not utter aloud: "Why did I walk into the kitchen? What did I intend to do here?"

Of course, I talk to Tommy often. I figure he's still interested in my minutiae, so his framed photo on my bedside table gets an earful. "You'll never believe what I did today, honey," I'll say. Behind the glass, he is permanently smiling. Two thumbs up, I imagine. Good enough for me.

Forty-Five:
Painting Furniture

The coffee table will be painted Sapphire Blue. Chris will also put a coat of Lime Rickey green on the kitchen table. Although their manufacturer, Sherwin-Williams, calls these colors Numbers 6963 and 6717, I prefer their more fanciful descriptions.

I need all the "fanciful" I can get. Once my house is sold, these two pieces of furniture, which will be jazzed up to disguise their scuff marks and worn spots, will accompany me to my eventual apartment. I figure the bright palette will add a bit of fun to smaller rooms.

Like judges in some weird beauty contest, my friends Karen the interior designer and Chris the decorative painter have joined me at my three-bedroom house to decide which pieces will fit in a very downsized space.

When I move out and bring the Sapphire Blue and Lime Rickey tables, the furniture I'm leaving behind will be part of a modest estate sale. Because I will gain some needed income and buyers seeking bargains will benefit, the ache I'm feeling during the furniture competition is lessened.

As we tour, I wonder: Do the pieces not making the cut feel wounded, like the two Room & Board living room couches that face each other? "Humph," I imagine them saying, "the measly coffee table she takes, but us she leaves behind."

To soothe the duo, whom I picture with their upholstered arms crossed in defiance, I send a silent message: *Listen, dears, Tommy and I absolutely loved you. But you're too big; you'd overwhelm the room. Even just one of you—and you know I could never split you up—wouldn't fit.*

I feel better when the secretary desk is among the finalists. Not my style, but Tommy brought it when he moved into my townhouse. "Nice, honey," I recall myself saying. As I ran my hands over the embossed design on the desk's front, I thought, *Where can I put this? It doesn't match anything else in the house.*

The quaint desk did win a spot in our guest bedroom, and that is where I once tucked myself away to write. I imitated a Victorian novelist and lowered its panel to reveal tiny cubbyholes and shelves that I filled with lined yellow pads, a variety of pens and pencils, books on "how to write," and draft after draft of heartfelt attempts.

"No paint," our trio of judges concludes as we eye the secretary desk. "It looks nice as is." It will go in my new bedroom, next to a window, and I will use the fold-down desk to hold a MacBook Air.

Alas, the various pieces of country-style furniture Tommy and I bought for our one-year experiment in Geneva, Illinois, will remain for the house sale. Did we really believe that the lovely home on one acre in picturesque Fox Valley would suit a couple who had lived their entire lives in the city? Perhaps my husband, as a gardener who immediately started planting, believed that. As for me, I discovered I could convince myself of anything, for a time.

Oh, if our furniture could tattle! The dining room table, with its one leaf extension, would tell of the evening that both my daughters, Faith and Jill, and their families, my ex-husband, and various friends and relatives joined us for a Passover dinner.

Tragically, three of those at the table have since died. Surprisingly, two partners have been exchanged for new ones. And, shockingly, one member has undergone a complete transformation. We knew none of that back then as we sat at the stretched-out table, laughing as the youngest guests performed in a Passover play. Will the table remember this rare, beautiful moment when my entire family was all in one place? Will it forgive me for not bringing it along?

One box spring and mattress, of three sets, will make the cut. Likely not the one Tommy and I slept in for sixteen years, as it is deepened on his side and indented on mine. Our Crate & Barrel dresser and one smaller bureau—both in their original wood finish—will move with me.

The chest of drawers on my husband's side, which still holds his exercise clothing, practice golf balls, broken alarm clock, and other items with his imprint, will be sold. First, though, I will remove all these things and pack them into a special box. Perhaps Chris will paint it. Sherwin-Williams's Number 6911, also known as Confident Yellow, sounds about right.

Forty-Six:
Roommate

This is what you cannot do when you have a roommate, especially if that person is a male: You cannot leave the door open when you go to the bathroom. You cannot assume that the extra-large T-shirt you've inherited from your deceased husband will disguise the fact that underneath you are not wearing a bra. And if said male roommate is the same age as your grown daughters, you cannot call him on his cell phone to learn why his thirty-minute trip to the grocery story has stretched beyond that time frame.

This is what you can do: You can ask him to alleviate your melancholy by accompanying you to three events that otherwise would've had you attending solo and, since you no longer own a car, can request he act as chauffeur in his. Importantly, you can advise him that the furnace filters need changing, show him how to pull down the ladder that leads to the one in the attic, and wait gratefully as he does the rickety climb.

So, on balance, it appears that the two weeks Chris is camping out in one of my guest bedrooms, while awaiting a move into his new apartment, is working out well. We made the unusual arrangement based on a barter deal. I provide his temporary housing; in exchange, Chris, a decorative painter, will jazz up two tables I plan to take to a River North rental. And, in a subsequent transaction, he will build and trade me a sawhorse desk for an aged computer.

"What do you know about him?" my daughter Jill asked when I was in the decision phase of the roommate deal. "Did you Google him?" Her tone of voice was familiar: What the hell was her batty mother getting into now?

"Karen vouched for him," I said. Karen is a longtime friend and interior designer who has aided several of my previous real estate moves. "She's known him for years and has referred his work to many of her clients," I added. "Very nice, quiet, dependable, she says."

Daughter Faith was the one who—in a terse text—ordered me to "wear a bra." Like her sister, once convinced I'd be appropriately attired and he'd been properly investigated, she supported my new roommate.

The offbeat pact was actually my idea. When Chris visited to give me an estimate on the paint job, he also mentioned he'd be moving to a new space. Somehow, the two-week housing void came up in the conversation, and the Jewish mother in me, who may have missed out by not having a third, male child, asked, "Where will you go?"

"Oh, a friend will rent me a room," he said. "I'll be fine."

"If it doesn't work out," I said, with my Leap Before You Look philosophy, "you can move in here."

The invitation may seem especially odd because, as you remember, I rebuffed any notion of boarders after my husband died, so I'm not sure what flipped the switch to make me welcome Chris. Was it my previously noted Jewish mother–ism and a longing for a male child? Or perhaps it was simply monetary: a chance to save writing a check for the refurbished furniture.

This is what I have landed on: my husband Tommy, abiding now in his heavenly abode, has become anxious about his widowed spouse. After all, he has known me for sixteen years, has witnessed my ineptness with household tools and appliances, and is aware of my jittery reaction to creaks and thumps.

Unable to care for me in his habitual manner, Tommy has sent in a substitute. My husband knows I would have rejected an older, paunchy type, as he himself was slender and fit most of his life, so he pitched a human I could accept. And Chris, with his black hair and partial Jewish genes, could pass for a relative.

"Good job," I tell Tommy in my nightly report. "My roommate is working out fine."

Then I could swear I heard back—or was it the wind?—"Always looking out for you, sweetheart. Never forget that, or the bra."

Forty-Seven:
Rolling the Dice

We have a contract for the sale of my house!

Although the closing doesn't occur until May 1, 2013, I've already signed a lease for my new apartment in River North that begins April 15. I'll use the week of the fifteenth to slowly move from one residence to another until my final departure date, April 22.

This early transition—sixteen days before I turn over the keys—is due to an April 28 sale of all of my belongings that are staying put. The company conducting the sale wants me, and a few furniture pieces, clothing, and personal items that are going with, to scram before a weeklong setup begins—hence the premature exit.

To many, my plan—as carefully thought out as a military maneuver—might seem risky. In fact, it was my lawyer's paralegal who warned, "You know there are always possibilities that a closing is held up." I didn't fault her caution; after all, it's her firm's job to protect me throughout the contract process.

"I understand the risks," I said. "I'm willing to take them. I have to move ahead."

I've often talked of my philosophy of Leap Before You Look. Now I'm adding another credo, which I will call Resist Limbo.

It was Chris, my temporary roommate, who originally urged a leap from on hold to full speed ahead. "You're ready to go," he said. "This house is too big for you. If this deal doesn't go through, it will certainly sell in a month."

Because Chris had been using his time with me to explore my neighborhood, I believed his words had weight. And since he'd had access to all the house had to offer, I believed he knew what he was talking about. "Essentially, you're a stranger," I said, "and you have faith in this house. Right?"

"No doubt," he said. "You should go."

That was all the incentive I needed.

"I'll be in tomorrow to sign the lease," I told the rental building's agent in an immediate phone call. He had held this particular apartment for me for over a month, and its time limit was growing closer. Because the rent and floor plan were exactly as I wanted, I didn't want to chance losing the unit.

"The twenty-eighth is solid" was the message I left in my next phone call. Again, the owner of the estate-sale company had been reserving the Sunday date for me, but I knew it was in jeopardy because of her increasing number of sales coming up in April.

As I was about to make my third call—to my daughters, to tell them of my speed-dialing decision—the paralegal called back. "No problems on the inspection," she said. "All looks good." She didn't bring up the closing risks; perhaps she now understood I couldn't be dissuaded. So I took the latest news as a sign I was moving in the right direction.

I can probably count on one hand the few rolls of the dice that haven't won me the jackpot; on the whole, my risks have turned out successfully. Let me relate stories of quick, and potentially dangerous, decisions:

After my first date with Tommy, we became a duo. He moved in with me just a month after that dinner at El Tapatio restaurant. We married within two years. We would have celebrated fifteen years January 13, 2013, but, sadly, my spouse was otherwise engaged.

As I've written many times, it appeared Tommy and I had little in common. Certainly, our marriage could be considered a major gamble. From religion to education to family obligations to bank accounts, we were at different ends of the spectrum. But my guy and I enjoyed the very same lifestyle: a peaceful home with a pet, evenings on the couch with TV, and respect for each other's hobbies. In short, I didn't have to golf, and he didn't have to love computers.

My career is one of a series of risky bets. In fact, some of my jobs lasted less than a year; others went a tad beyond that time frame. Here's the map: Bernard Ury & Associates; Elaine Soloway Public Relations; Public Communications, Inc.; Mayor Jane Byrne; CPS Superintendent Ruth Love; Jasculca/Terman; Elaine Soloway Public Relations; Apple Store; and then—drum roll, please—back to my own business as Elaine Soloway Consulting.

Did this dicey route stigmatize me as someone with a short attention span? I prefer seeing myself as a selective seizer of opportunity.

There's no predicting my latest gamble will pay off. Certainly, glitches could arise before, or at, the closing. But, once again, I'll take my chances. Leap Before You Look, Resist Limbo, and now: Trust.

Forty-Eight:
A Dollhouse, Part Two

After my father died in 1959, my mother, Min, his forty-five-year-old widow, and I moved into a garden apartment. At least, that's what the real estate listing called it. Basement was more like it.

Mom had a knack for decorating and soon transformed the dark and occasionally damp space into what visitors called a "dollhouse." Needlework that she had handcrafted hung on walls in the living room and in the one bedroom.

Despite her beautifying, the apartment was more subterranean than floral. The back door opened into the building's laundry room, and in the living room, when I sat on the plastic-covered couch and looked out the window, I could see the feet of other tenants as they walked past.

I recalled those mother-daughter dollhouse days after I, a seventy-four-year-old widow, moved into my 615-square-foot apartment on April 15, 2013. Although I covered the experience in my roman à clef e-book, *She's Not the Type*, I thought it worthwhile to revisit that episode and description.

Here's how my own downsizing began. Following Tommy's death in November 2012, I had at first planned to accede to advice offered to the bereaved: don't make a major move for at least a year.

But this obligatory timetable weighed on me. "I'm so discouraged," I said to my daughter Faith. She was in town for

Tommy's memorial, and I was using her as a sympathetic ear.

She put her hand on my shoulder. Her face had a worried look. This was not a typical mood for her mother. Throughout my husband's illness, hospitalization, hospice, and death, I had stayed strong and confident.

"It's only natural," Faith said. "Look at all you've been through."

"No, it's not that," I said. "It's that I see such a dismal future. I'll have to rent out half the garage and turn our two spare bedrooms into housing for boarders. That's the only way I can see handling my bills."

I went to bed that evening, leaving my daughter uneasy at my dispirited state. But in the middle of the night, I woke with a thought: *I don't have to listen to widow advice that doesn't fit me. I don't have to stay in the house.*

In the morning, Faith headed straight to my home office, prepared to console me once again. Instead, she found me searching the web for downtown, luxury high-rise rental apartments.

"Look," I shouted to her. "Swimming pool, business center, and exercise room!"

At first, my daughter was alarmed by this sudden mood swing. "What happened, Mom?" she said. "Last night, you were—"

"I don't have to stay," I said. "I can sell the house and move to a smaller place, one that I can handle. No snow shoveling, lawn mowing, worrying about downspouts, sump pumps, furnaces, water heaters. All the stuff I don't understand in the first place. And I won't have to share the garage or bedrooms."

And that's what I did. To both of my daughters' relief, I put the house on the market and found my version of a dollhouse. But, unlike the one I lived in with Mom, this one has me on the nineteenth floor, so no feet obstruct my view, which to the north overlooks the river and to the east, downtown.

Although I lack my mother's craftiness, all of the paintings that I love now grace the walls of my new home and feel just right. And with Chris's help, I have a petite office for my business that sports a Sapphire Blue desk and bench, both cut down to my size.

Best of all, I can walk through my building's garage to my

exercise club, which, for an early-morning person like me, is a special treat. Neither rain nor snow will prevent my workouts.

In daily texts to my daughters, I have written, "Worked out, met my friend for breakfast, had a massage."

And "I'm living the life you dreamed of for me."

Although I can't see their faces in Boston and Los Angeles, nor hear their voices, I interpret their texted responses of "So happy. You deserve it. Can't wait to see your new place" to mean they're as satisfied as I am with my swift choice.

Now I wonder: In her afterlife abode, how does Mom view my digs? And my dear Tommy—how does he feel about my leaving our house?

"Perfect," I can hear Mom saying, and I see two thumbs up from Tommy. I believe they are both relieved, and at peace, to find me cocooned in my own dollhouse.

Forty-Nine:
My Psyche and Its Five Stages

In the past few weeks, my psyche has been on a roller coaster. I've counted five stages that lifted, dropped, and finally steadied me.

The Euphoric phase began when I prepared to move into my new apartment. I breezed through my to-do list: hire a mover, arrange for a house sale, unpack boxes with the help of a best friend, submit maintenance request for paintings to be hung, renew membership at adjacent health club.

As prepared as I was for Euphoria, I failed to brace myself for the next stage and wound up capsized by Grief. This is what happened: The estate sale of left-behinds was over. I thought it wise to return and check out the house before the buyer's walkthrough that was to occur on the morning of the real estate closing.

"Why are you going back?" one of my daughters asked.

"I just have to be sure all is okay for the walkthrough," I said.

"Do you think you can handle it?"

"I don't know," I said.

I took the Blue Line from my apartment, then walked the short blocks to my house. I was only halfway there when I felt myself crumbling.

"Will you go with me?" I said to a neighbor as she was getting into her car. "I'm going to check out the house, and I don't think I can do it alone."

"I'm on my way to pick up the kids," she said, "but I'll get my husband."

I stood on the sidewalk, sinking lower each minute, as she raced into the house and returned with her husband. He grabbed my hand.

"I thought I could handle it," I said, already weeping.

"No problem," he said.

When we arrived at my front door, my neighbor handed me off to the owner of the estate-sale company, who was awaiting the pickup of my upright piano.

"I'll take it from here," she said, and opened her arms for my collapse.

As I hung on to her, I viewed the empty house, now devoid of furniture, artwork, clothing, pantry or refrigerator goods, and I sobbed.

The emptiness and finality summoned the same anguish I experienced with my husband's death.

"Get it all out," she said.

By the time I left our house for the last time, I had recovered. I reversed my route and returned to my apartment.

Two days later, a text arrived from my real estate broker: "The walkthrough went fine, no problems."

"Thank God!" I sent back. "I was on pins and needles." Because I had rolled the dice and moved out before the closing, I was especially grateful to enter this stage, Relief.

A few hours later, a phone call from the same person. "Congratulations," he led off. "I wanted to be the first to tell you: the closing is over; all went well. You're no longer a homeowner."

I sent texts to my daughters and friends who were awaiting the outcome of the closing: "'Tis done!"

Their responses came immediately: "Congratulations!" "You must be so relieved!" "Yay!"

But instead of joining the glee chorus, I had an odd feeling of—how shall I say it?—anticlimax. Where was the euphoria I had felt when I moved, preclosing, to my new apartment? Where was the relief from the first text reporting a successful walkthrough?

I realized then that those positive emotions had been first put into play with Tommy's death. His absence, the void, the empty house, the finality, would forever tinge these pleasurable feelings.

"You can pick up your check" came the next electronic message—this from the paralegal who had worked on the deal.

As I walked from the lawyer's office to my financial manager's, with the check from the house sale proceeds tucked inside my tote, I felt myself entering yet another stage: Pride. I had done it. I had made the decision to put the house on the market. I had successfully, with my broker's aid, negotiated a price that brought a bounce to my retirement account. I had moved and unpacked and was already settled in my new home.

My roller coaster ride is easing toward the finish line. I'm calling this stage Acceptance. Not as heady as Euphoria, much better than Grief, a companion to Relief and Pride, and an emotion that I pray will keep me company as I move through even more stages of this new life.

Fifty:
Coed Majoring in Phys Ed

I never went away to college. When I graduated from Roosevelt High School, my parents couldn't afford to send me downstate to the University of Illinois, or to other places my wealthier classmates chose. So, every day, I took the CTA to Roosevelt University, which had granted me a partial scholarship. And, following classes, I again rode the trains to a part-time job.

As I look back, this was hardly an idyllic undergrad campus experience. But because my best friend, Ruth, also went to Roosevelt, and because I received a great education, I didn't feel deprived.

Now, in this new chapter of my rookie widow life, a bit of imaginary campus life seems to be emerging. Often I feel as if I were a freshman, away from home for the first time, majoring in physical education.

I was explaining my theory to Ruth, who is still my best friend after all these years. "You're right on one count," she said. "We both went straight from our parents' homes to our marriages. There was no period of time when we were on our own."

One of my daughters, to whom I also gave this hypothesis, disagreed: "What about the time you and Dad separated?" she said. "You lived alone then."

"Somehow, this is different," I said. "You two girls were still in Chicago and stopped in often enough that I felt as if I were living the same life. Just without him."

I've been musing about this sensation of a freshman year and believe some of it may be related to home furnishings, some to the youthful population in my apartment building, and some to my more-active life.

Because my apartment is a convertible studio, with a bedroom behind a sliding door, the queen-size bed that Tommy and I shared was too large. So I dropped down a size to a full, to better suit my fictitious dorm room.

Also, the new, bright paint colors that adorn my kitchen table, coffee table, and hall table make them appear not only brand new but also purchased at kicky IKEA. Surely, that's where true coeds find their furniture.

I revealed the other half of my conjecture—my chosen major— to another daughter. "So, phys ed?" she said. There was a pause while she likely recalled her mother's previous attempts to learn how to swim, my start-and-stop gym memberships, and my lack of coordination.

"Should I expect to see you in a league?" she asked. "Uniform with logo on the back?"

I smiled and accepted the skepticism, which I knew was trimmed in pride. Both daughters are my biggest supporters in my recent sad-and-swift journey from wife to widow, from homeowner to apartment dweller.

"No leagues," I said. "But, I work out every day. I take yoga three days a week, have a personal trainer one day, do the workout on my own two more days, take swim lessons, and paddle by myself whenever I can fit it in."

"Good for you, Momma," she said. I'd like to think that a vision of an active parent striving to keep fit, who has elected to live in a tower of mostly thirty-somethings, rather than with peers in assisted living, would delight my kid.

In my imaginary college life, I've also decided that I live on a campus. You see, the health club where I work out is attached to my apartment building, so I have the sense that I'm trekking the quadrangle.

Here's another aspect of university life that supports my theme: class assignments and homework. In the real world, I'm still operating my public relations business and my sidelines of coaching writing and using Apple mobile devices.

While my phys ed workouts are a priority, there's a danger of neglecting revenue-producing work, sort of like flunking out. And this time around, without a sympathetic university to grant me funds, hitting the books is essential. But without frat parties, sorority mixers, and other late-night revelry, I should be able to pass my freshman year.

Of course, if I wanted to bring my make-believe world closer to a true collegiate experience, there should be a roommate sharing my space. While a corporeal buddy would be ideal, this coed will settle for framed photographs of a beloved husband. Like me, my Tommy missed the campus experience. Let's try this together, sweetheart:

We're loyal to you, Illinois,
We're "Orange and Blue," Illinois,
We'll back you to stand 'gainst the best in the land,
For we know you have sand, Illinois. Rah! Rah!

Fifty-One:
Re-couching the Potato

I'm on the couch, watching an episode of *Castle*, when I say aloud, "This is a fun show, Tommy. I wonder why I didn't watch it with you."

Of course, there is no reply from my spouse, as he has been dead for over six months. But, like many widows, I regularly engage in such one-sided conversations.

I continue, "I know you're getting a kick out of my being back on a couch. They tried to pull me off, but the routines you and I treasured are winning out."

The "they" I'm referring to includes my daughters and my friends, who derided my married couch-potato lifestyle. It's likely they blamed my reluctance to venture out after hours on either my husband's preference and my adherence to his wishes or, later, during his illness, on my wanting to be on hand for his care.

While some of this is true, I must now confess: Tommy wouldn't have cared if I'd left him to join friends for an evening out. On the few occasions I did this, I'd return, flop onto his couch, and jokingly say, "Don't make me go out again."

"You belong home with me and the Pooker!" he'd say. Buddy, our golden retriever, would be tucked in next to Tommy, so I'd have to squeeze myself in between man and dog to make my silly announcement. Of course, that scenario occurred before aphasia robbed my spouse of speech and when Buddy—who somehow became the Pooker—hadn't succumbed to his fourteen-year-old canine ailments.

My life obviously changed when Tommy died. With his presence not overriding decisions, I opted to try to fulfill the wishes of They. So I booked theater events and dinners out with friends. In long-distance calls and on Facebook status updates, I trumpeted, "The potato is becoming un-couched." At once, those championing an exit from my nightly horizontal TV-watching habit lauded me.

And when I sold our house and moved to a downtown apartment, my support team concluded, "Now that you're in the city, you'll find it so much easier to go out in the evenings. Restaurants, theaters, movie houses, all nearby." With my interests at heart, they likely envisioned me dolling up nightly, slipping on high-heeled shoes, enveloping myself in new, not-black-T-shirt-and-not-blue-jeans clothing.

Alas, a leopard doesn't change her spots and you can't teach an old dog new tricks. Take your pick of these animal-themed clichés. After a month in my new urban lifestyle, with a vibrant city and night lights summoning from my floor-to-ceiling windows, here I am, plopped on my solo couch and even finding new TV shows to watch. I offer a few reasons:

1) I love TV. Tommy and I had a roster of shows—primarily police and medical procedurals, with a few sitcoms thrown in—that I taped so we could watch them together during our 7:00–8:00 p.m. viewing. I've since stretched that time to begin at six because I've added Netflix and Apple TV and am catching up on missed programs.

2) I'm an early-to-bed-and-early-to-rise kind of a gal. I've been this way for as long as I can remember. As proof, there are black-and-white photos of me slumbering atop folded arms on banquet tables at weddings and bar mitzvahs. So, like those metal doors that seal run-down storefronts, my lids fold at 8:00 p.m.

3) Because I am much more active during the day, I require evenings at home to recharge. I live adjacent to a health club, and I exercise most mornings. There's a Trader Joe's, a Whole Foods, a Mariano's, and a Target within walking distance. These frequent two-mile round trips, accompanied by age and arthritis, demand relief.

4) I have lunch dates nearly every day. Friends are eager to see my new place, so we've been booking meals at nearby restaurants. One restaurant meal per day is fun; two is overkill.

So now, in my adorable urban apartment, with a view of the Chicago River and skyscrapers, I'm on my couch with a dinner tray atop my stretched-out legs. While my loved ones might be disappointed in this turn of events, I know of someone who's delighted. "Move over," I imagine him saying. So I do, and at the same time, I make room for the Pooker.

Fifty-Two:
The Men in My Life

I've unpacked the tin tubes, plastic posts, and curved tops from the skinny box that has arrived from Walmart. The directions for the shoe rack appear fairly simple: attach this to that, then that to this, and, finally, remove scrambled shoes from the floor of my bedroom closet and set them neatly on the gizmo. Alas, my assembly looked like a wacky Lego, rather than the structure the carton's front promised.

Ramir to the rescue; in less than five minutes, he unscrewed and repositioned all of the parts until they comprised a replica of the image. Ramir—along with George, Greg, José, and Roberto, who are members of the maintenance crew in my Kingsbury Plaza apartment building—has smoothly taken over the help-mate role once performed by my husband and several men who lived on my block on Dakin Street.

Back then, when Tommy and I lived in our house, John topped the team who cared for us. Even before my spouse became ill, when he was still able to mow the grass or shovel the walk, John would beat him to it.

"Honey," I'd say, "I hear a snowblower outside. Do you think it's John?"

We'd both go to the window, open the drapes, and wave as we saw our neighbor steering through white mounds on our front walk on his way to our driveway. While John was the überneighbor, there were other males who came to our aid as well.

"Whatever you need, any time of day" was what Casey said as the ambulance drivers were bringing Tommy up the stairs after our ride from Northwestern Memorial Hospital. Then Casey placed a yellow Post-in in my hands, with his cell phone number on it.

Joél on Dakin Street asked how he could help after I had hip surgery. "My car needs maintenance," I told him. "Give me the keys," he said.

During the twelve days my husband was in hospice, upstairs in the bed with railings on both sides, his longtime buddy Randy visited several times a week to rake leaves and declutter the downspouts.

After Tommy died and I sold our house and moved to my apartment building, friends who were experienced renters said, "You won't have to worry about lawns or snow anymore. And if anything needs fixing, you just call maintenance."

And I did. At first, my requests were basic: replace a dead lightbulb, unclog the bathroom sink's drain, and coax a stubborn icemaker. But the new men in my life have far surpassed those everyday appeals. With care and precision, members of the staff have hung all of the two dozen paintings on the walls of my convertible studio.

And it was Ramir who was at the door after this request: "I have a Hoover upright vacuum cleaner, and I can't figure out how to put it together." As I stood nearby, feeling like a dazzled intern watching a surgeon, Ramir studied the carton's image and quickly performed the operation. "Let's test it first," he said. He plugged the cord into the wall socket and, after the first loud hum, showed me how to steer it. Then he stood by to be certain I could manage the hefty machine on my own.

"Can I give you something?" I asked him then—and again, at the latest shoe-rack assembly—for I knew these tasks didn't really fall under the category of maintenance. But this new man in my life waved away my question and was quickly out the door.

When Tommy was well, which he was the majority of our sixteen years together, he was our family handyman, making frequent trips to our basement to select a tool from his wooden worktable or a nail, screw, hook, or other tidbit from his wall-mounted pegboard.

As his health deteriorated and his aspirations evaporated, and after I bequeathed the table, tools, and pegboard to our good neighbor John, I held on to one hammer, one screwdriver, and a pair of pliers, believing I'd need them in a future life.

I've used each gadget occasionally: to pound the top of a stubborn jar of pickles, to open a key ring and add a store's loyalty card, and to twist off the top of a bottle of nail polish. But thanks to the new men in my life—who have accepted all of the responsibilities the guys on Dakin Street and my own beloved handyman once handled—that's all this trio of tools will likely be asked to do.

Fifty-Three:
Green Nails and Other Acts
of Rebellion

"I know you hate them," I say to Tommy, "but when you died, you forfeited your vote on my nails."

If my husband were still alive, I would never have handed over a bottle of Estée Lauder's Absinthe to the manicurist. Tommy made it clear that he found shades other than natural, beige, or a subtle pink garish.

It was easy to go along with his preferences when his wishes were earthbound, because my spouse of fourteen years was a dear. "He makes me feel as if I walk on water," I often told people who were curious about the differences in our religion, bank accounts, family relationships, and levels of education. And let me tell you, that's a sentiment not easy to come by.

There were other habits that Tommy brought into this second marriage that I tolerated, even when, toward the end of his life, his illness magnified them.

At first I tried. "Honey," I'd say, putting a hand on his arm, "sit. You can clear up the counter after we finish eating." But he'd touch my cheek—a gesture I took as, "You're cute, but it's not going to happen."

So, while I started in on the meal I prepared (that was our division of labor: I was the cook; he was the bottle washer), watching a rerun of *The Andy Griffith Show*, Tommy would rise, leaving his food to turn cold, as he put various utensils in the dishwasher, replaced the menu's ingredients in the refrigerator or cupboard, and wiped down the countertops. By the time he returned to his chair, I was usually on my last mouthful.

Now, you guessed it, in my new life sans spouse, everything—dishes, ingredients, serving spoons, and more—remains out until I feel like cleaning up. I imagine Tommy and these waiting kitchen objects engaged in conversation: "Can you believe it?" the tossed dishtowel says to my husband. "The woman you thought walked on water has become a slob."

"How long do you think she's going to leave us sitting here?" I could swear the frying pan adds. "Doesn't she realize the grease is going to harden and make my cleanup that much tougher?"

While those bossy things are jabbering about me, my resurrected husband is smiling. If I place him in the conjured scene while he still had a voice, he'd say, "I had a feeling that would happen. She's a sweetheart, but without me around, I can see how she'd get sloppy."

Now, if it were later in his life, when his aphasia erased speech, Tommy would just shake his head and turn the thumbs of each hand down—a sign of displeasure that is now bouncing off my slovenly shoulders.

I ignore my pretend cast of characters who are casting aspersion and finish my meal. With my viewing partner gone, I have switched television programs. Sheriff Andy has given way to Mr. White, of the hit series *Breaking Bad*. Also, instead of kitchen-table viewing, in my new apartment, I've transitioned to couch-with-dinner-tray-on-lap.

I'm not certain if this counts as a genuine act of rebellion, because Tommy and I weren't watchers of the drama back then. But the violence and drug themes might have put him off. Remember, this is a man who prefers nails in neutral shades rather than tropical colors.

This part, though, is definitely treasonous. I stack the dinner dishes in the sink, intending to place them in the dishwasher—maybe this night, maybe tomorrow morning, maybe even tomorrow evening.

With an evil smile, likely inspired by the TV show, I turn to the figments of my imagination and say, "I don't care what you think. The dishes can wait."

Everybody but Tommy receives this declaration aghast. "Has she fallen this low?" I believe the empty wineglass says to the salad plate. Then the crabbing crew turns to my husband, expecting equal derision and disbelief.

But he is laughing. A subtle, sweet laugh, as if he is in on the joke. "Relax," he says. "Give her time. She's like a kid let out of school, testing her independence. Just watch—in a few weeks, her kitchen will look more like ours did when I was in charge."

Tommy may be right, for I unwittingly just returned the salad dressing to the fridge pre-tuck-in. Oh well—the rebellion was fun while it lasted, but the green nails definitely stay.

Fifty-Four:
Flights of Fancy

I knew it had to be Tommy playing tricks. It happened as I was preparing for a visit to Los Angeles—my first travel from my new rental apartment. On the day before my trip, I opened my wallet to take out my driver's license. My plan was to clip the license to my boarding pass, which, in my obsessively organized mind, would ease my passage through security.

Gadzooks, the license was gone! With my heart racing, I dropped to the couch and retraced my steps. Where was the last place I had used the license? Was there an establishment I had visited that required this extra identification in order to make a credit card purchase?

Then I remembered: one day, feeling nostalgic about all of the changes in my life and pining for my deceased husband, I had switched the driver's license, which was under the clear plastic slot, to another spot in my wallet. Now, instead of my government-issued face greeting me, it was a color photo of our wedding portrait.

But the driver's license edge wasn't peeking out from any other slot, like my credit cards were. Where had I put it? Then I jabbed my fingers behind the photo, and voilà. I was certain I had put my license in its own niche, where I could easily notice and extract it, but somehow, someone—and I am now pointing fingers—had hidden it tightly behind the two-by-three-inch picture.

In my flight of fancy, prior to the actual airplane I was to

151

board the next day, I decided Tommy was having a bit of fun with me. When he was alive, he often scoffed at my habit of hyper-preparation. For example, two weeks before any takeoff, I'd lay everything out in stacks next to my open suitcase. This way, I could add or delete as my departure day neared.

When he'd walk past the room and spot the gaping luggage, he'd say, "We're not going for two weeks. What's the rush?"

"This makes it easier," I'd say, which made sense to me, but to my casual husband, who refused to pack until the night before, or morning of, my regimen deserved ridicule.

After further daydreaming, though, I decided Tommy was also trying to remind me of the trips we had taken together. He wanted to be certain I wouldn't allow those memories to fade.

With my departed husband prodding my subconscious, I paused preparations to conjure up those long-ago vacations. As if I were assembling a jigsaw puzzle, I positioned images, expressions, and other mementos side by side until I could see a fuller picture.

First it was words that came to mind, likely because I was grateful for the years Tommy still had speech. "Mind the gap," I could hear him saying. We were standing on a London platform, awaiting public transit. On that trip, we visited Buckingham Palace, Harrods, and other typical tourist spots. And in my reverie, I also remembered "punting on the Cam," held over from a visit with friends in Cambridge, which Tommy enjoyed repeating for weeks after we returned home.

We toured Italy—the Spanish Steps in Rome, the destroyed city of Pompeii, the hillside villages of the Amalfi Coast—and dined in restaurants the guides promised were frequented by locals. I was still able to capture bits and pieces, but so much of those travel memories had been slipping away with each passing year.

"Yes, those were wonderful," I told Tommy aloud. "I'm so happy we were able to take them together." I noted that my husband, in this celestial cameo, hadn't brought up our last mutual trip, to Boston. I assumed he didn't want to remind me of the difficulties after he had lost speech and his brain suggested to him a false bravado.

Had Tommy held on to some resentment from that episode? Would that explain his current trick? No, I prefer to think my first notion was on target: my dear husband was just sending me a message. "Have a safe trip," he was saying, "and don't forget me." As if.

Fifty-Five:
Empty-Nest Syndrome, Part Two

I had narrowed my search to synagogues whose online descriptions contained code words that met my criteria: inclusion, equality of women, welcoming to gays and lesbians. As I scrutinized their monthly bulletins, I imagined myself sitting in a Torah class, debating the text's contemporary relevance. Would that satisfy a current tug?

Maybe a Sabbath service at another house of worship? Could that reignite my lapsed faith? Or would a film or book group provide stimulation and challenge? A social-justice program focused on immigration? How about that one?

The quest began to feel familiar, so I closed the cover of my laptop and moved to the couch for further investigation. It was there, sinking into the furniture's comforting cushions, with my eyes shut, that I found my mind free to flip the pages of the calendar backward. Days, weeks, months, years reversed, until I reached 1988. That's where my tour ended. I was likely, once again, suffering from empty-nest syndrome, albeit with very different losses.

I pin my first experience with the malady on the gloom I felt after my two daughters moved from living at home to their own apartments. But that wasn't the excuse I used to cajole my first husband. My addiction to my girls, and his feelings of being lower down on my list of beloveds, were already causing frays in our twenty-eight-year marriage. So I opted for a project I thought could bring us closer together and perhaps fill the void my absent offspring had left.

"I want to join a synagogue," I told my husband. We were living in a posh condominium off of Michigan Avenue and were seated at the breakfast table with a view of the lake and other high-rise buildings.

"Why now?" he asked as he divided the morning paper— sports for him, local news for me.

"The High Holidays are coming up, and I don't want to feel left out," I said. "I don't want to feel dumb anymore." This was believable, and it remained the excuse I gave to others who questioned my synagogue search and my timing.

"I'll do the investigating, and if I find one that feels comfortable, you can check it out," I said.

We landed at the Jewish Reconstructionist Congregation (JRC) in Evanston. With its charismatic rabbi's encouragement, I joined the board of directors and embarked on a yearlong study to have an adult bat mitzvah.

My plan worked. My husband joined the synagogue's choir, accompanied me to Saturday-morning services, and lifted his tenor voice in ritual song during the celebration of my late-to-the-game coming-of-age ceremony.

Then he left me for another woman.

Feeling like a third wheel, and possibly an object of pity for those who knew my story, I dropped my JRC membership. Occasionally I returned, and when I married Tommy, I brought him to a special service. But my second husband had his own, Lutheran lapses and, while he encouraged my bond to my roots, had no interest in joining me. So I slowly let Judaism seep away, until this current search.

While my first attack of empty-nest syndrome was brought on by my daughters' departure, I realize now this second episode is due to a combination of losses. Consider: within a period of six months, Tommy and I soothed our golden retriever as the dog took his last breath; then, three months later, it was my husband who died after being diagnosed with throat cancer.

Then I added to these losses by—in what seemed like a

flash—selling our house and moving out of a neighborhood where the dog and the spouse and I all lived happily for thirteen years with model neighbors.

While my swift action was intended to lift depression and establish myself in a new, urban lifestyle—and in many ways the relocation has accomplished this—that blue feeling that accompanied my daughters' leave-taking has begun to creep in.

How to fill the void? Will a particular synagogue help me find new faith and relieve the sadness? But then I consider those old "third wheel" feelings that arose for me as a solo amid families and couples. Would I be at ease in pews of longtime members up to speed with one another and with liturgy?

Perhaps I should instead postpone the search, slow down, and sit with the inevitable sorrow that has been my recent visitor. Staying put—a new challenge for me.

Fifty-Six:
Head Trip

"Just put it on my credit card," I say to the American Airlines agent at the gate.

I'm pleased with myself. I have gotten to LaGuardia early enough to catch a flight that will get me home several hours sooner than my original ticket.

As I move to the back of the line of passengers on the jetway, I look at my ticket and again pat myself on the back. "Aisle seat, row eleven, extra legroom!" I say aloud. I'm not worried my fellow flyers will question my glee, because they'd certainly empathize with this great spot.

But my outspoken declaration must've roused my husband, who, since his own flight departure, has been residing in my head and engaging me in frequent conversations.

"I don't know why you're feeling so proud of yourself," I imagine him saying. "You just spent $75 to get this earlier flight, and that's on top of the $75 you spent to change airports."

I'm not surprised to hear Tommy's view, because my recent shifts and credit card action were two hot spots in our otherwise mellow marriage. As an example of his steadfastness, my husband lived in the same apartment for several decades. His bride, though, counted thirteen changes of residence before we met, and two more, post–Las Vegas nuptials.

In the second area of major spousal differences, Tommy worked at jobs with modest salaries yet managed to enter our

157

marriage with an admirable savings account. Me? I supplemented my income with a home equity line of credit, and even when my tax advisor warned me that I would likely outlive my money, I did little to change my practice.

"Is it the extra $150 that's bothering you, honey?" I ask the curmudgeon accompanying me along the gangplank. "You of all people should understand that life is unpredictable, and hanging at the airport, wasting precious time, is crazy."

What I don't point out is this: Less than a year ago, who could have forecasted how little time Tommy had left on Earth before he took up residence in my head? We should've taken that trip to the Greek Islands we talked about. Or Japan. Oh, there were a number of places that were on our Someday list. And now Tommy is relegated to being my fanciful traveling partner.

My spouse is quiet as I find my aisle seat, and when I enlist a sturdy male to hoist my carry-on to the overhead bin. This, of course, was my muscular husband's task on the trips we did take together. In his absence, I pull my little-old-lady act and stand helpless until someone conjures his granny and comes to my aid.

Once I'm settled, with my seat belt securely fastened, Tommy starts up again. "So, why Kennedy instead of LaGuardia?" he asks. "If you had chosen this airport in the first place, you could've saved $150 in change fees, plus the $20 difference in cab fares."

I was wondering when he was going to get around to that major gaffe. I have my answer at the ready: I'll blame someone else.

"Well, I put the query on my Facebook page and . . . "

Do I see my spouse shaking his head? I realize I have walked into a third breach in our harmonious life. While I own every Apple device Steve Jobs dreamed up, I couldn't get my husband to desire an email address. His only interest in technology came when he'd haul a kitchen chair to my home office and glare over my shoulder as I opened website after website, trying to find his perfect golf club.

"Okay, honey," I say. "I know you don't like Facebook or understand my obsession with it, but normally my friends have submitted very good responses to my questions. For example . . . "

I stop before I can list the successful recommendations that clearly outnumbered this last, erroneous answer of Kennedy over LaGuardia. "Okay, maybe I should've done more research," I say. "It was a learning experience. Next trip in, I'll have the right answer."

Tommy is silent. Have I wounded him? I shouldn't have mentioned visits to New York. I jump in before his voice returns to my head. "This trip was great," I say, "but nothing like our jaunt to the Big Apple. I didn't do any of the memorable things we did together. No Central Park, no Ellis Island, no Tenement Museum."

As the airplane lifts from the runway, I close my eyes to recall that wonderful weekend we shared. Do I slumber? It's possible, because Tommy quiets down, too, likely satisfied I haven't forgotten.

Fifty-Seven:
Body Type

I watch as she moves closer to him. When her body meets his, she lifts her arms to wrap them around his neck. She raises her chin to smile. He looks down at her, circles her waist with his arms, and then offers a happy grin.

My paper cup of iced decaf is cold in my hand, so I shift from staring at the young couple to finding a seat in the café. I lower my tote bag onto the empty chair next to me, extract my cell phone, and check email messages. But soon enough, I return my gaze to the couple. They are chatting while still deep in the hug.

This is what I miss from my marriage, from my husband: the toe-to-toe enveloping, the hug. I wonder, does she get to inhale the scent of a freshly laundered shirt, as I did when I closed in on Tommy? Does her boyfriend's shirt smell of Target's lemon-scented detergent? Tommy's did.

Although my husband was decades older than the lad in my vision, his frame and strong body were similar. When I met Tommy, on the street where we both lived, my first thought was, *Not my body type.* He was about five foot nine, tall enough for a shrimp like me, but had no fat, no rolls plumping his belly. "Nothing to hang on to," I complained to my friend after a few early dates.

The short, tubby, white-haired Santa Claus type, sans the red suit, was what I was going for after my divorce from my first husband, who, at six feet and skinny, towered over me. I didn't need

Dr. Freud to diagnose that my predilection for rotundness was based on my father, the parent who called me his princess.

Before I met Tommy, I found a boyfriend during that Bermuda Triangle period of my life—between divorce and remarriage—who perfectly fit my body-type requirements. He was short and fat, had gray hair, and even smoked around the clock, like dear, departed Dad. While the cigarettes, fast and careless driving, unhealthy eating, and intense friendships with other women should've sounded alarms, I was too smitten to think clearly.

Fortunately, my father's doppelgänger settled on another woman whom he fancied more than me. I lamented for a bit but eventually realized I was fortunate for having dodged a lifestyle that likely would've had me growing infirm and fat.

When nonsmoking, tip-top-shape Tommy came into my life, I quickly tossed out my previous preferred body type and came to love the one I married. Of course, my husband's other prized features helped me dump doughy. Tommy was low maintenance and helpful around the house, had interests that matched mine, and, most important, thought I walked on water.

Not long after my sighting of the hugging couple, I told my daughter, "I'm not ready to date, and I can't imagine sharing my new life with anyone, but I miss spooning. It's a bedtime perk I pine for."

"Try a pillow," she said. "Get a king-size one, place it vertically in Tommy's spot, and cuddle up."

In the bedding department of Macy's, I had my choice: down-feather combinations, foam, polyester fiberfill, memory foam, and latex. Prices varied. When the salesperson was out of sight, I lifted each pillow and hugged it to my body. As in the children's fable, one was too soft, another too hard, and one—although not perfect—would do.

Along with my pillow selection, I bought a set of king-size pillowcases. I washed the pair in Target's lemon-scented laundry detergent and then slipped one over my husband's proxy.

At night, as I clasped the pillow to my body, I knew my arrangement would be a poor second to the real thing. The body type turned out to be flawed, too cushy where it should've been muscled, too short where it should've been a few heads taller. But the freshly laundered pillowcase conjured a fragrance that improved my tableau.

With my imagination urging me on, I whispered to the pillow, "Love you, Tommy." This was my half of the duet we played out each night. In my head, the one now deep into my polyester fiber-fill, I could hear his response: "Love you, too!"

The pillow, which soon morphed into my perfect body type, and I grew drowsy; then we both surrendered to sleep.

Fifty-Eight:
Swell Party

"So, what are you planning for your seventy-fifth?" a friend asked.

"I don't think I want a party," I said. "I'll declare the entire month of August my birthday, and I'll let friends take me out to dinner."

"Sounds like a good plan," she said. We were on the phone, so I couldn't see her expression, but her tone was skeptical.

"I'll save money and avoid bruising those I don't include in a big bash," I said, trying to convince her, and myself.

But was it really a good plan? What if the once-in-a-lifetime occasion drifted away and I came to regret the absence of a party? And despite the several friends who volunteered to host individual birthday meals, my idea was beginning to feel tepid. Even depressing.

As I continued to muse about my approaching big day, I decided to pitch the question to Tommy. "What do you think, honey?" I said aloud. No one else was in my apartment when I launched our dialogue, so I didn't have to fear skepticism or derision. "Expensive party or a series of dinners?"

I waited a few beats to conjure my deceased husband, but, soon enough, I could feel his presence. "This bed is too small" were his first words. I was propped upright on two pillows in the new full-size bed I had purchased for my small apartment. Tommy's assessment was coming from the empty side of the bed.

"It fits my life here," I said. "But let's get to the question at hand. Do you agree it's better to ditch a party and save money and bruised feelings?"

I expected a significant yes, because for his seventy-fifth, we went to a restaurant with two other couples. I had offered a party, but my husband, who shunned the spotlight and frivolous expenditures, had declined.

"You should have a party," I was certain I heard him saying. "And I'll throw it for you."

I placed my hand on the bare linen and then on the pillow that I hugged each night, pretending it was Tommy. He continued, "Ask Barry if he'll open our favorite restaurant for you on a Monday, when he's usually closed."

"Smoque? The barbecue place in our old neighborhood?" I said.

Because I was directing this movie in my head, I could pause it at any point and insert flashbacks. I saw Tommy and me entering the restaurant, just days after it opened. Barbecue, a few blocks from our house! I was in heaven.

Although my husband was a vegetarian, he was satisfied with salad, mac and cheese, baked beans, french fries, and peach cobbler, while his wife alternated between ribs, brisket, and chicken. He knew my addiction to this menu and, in his love for me, put Smoque at the top of the list when I asked him for a lunch choice.

In my film, I saw calendar pages flip quickly as Tommy and I remained patrons of our neighborhood joint. As his brain degeneration progressed, we developed a ritual. As soon as we entered, he'd head for the cooler, pluck a cola, and then proceed to our regular table. I'd go to the counter, order his veggie sides, then add my meat choice of the day.

Tommy was in charge of salt and pepper packets and plastic silverware, which he'd pick up on his route back to our seats. Within thirty minutes, without my husband having to struggle to find words or conversation, we'd be on our way home.

"What about the money?" I posed to my apparition. "It's really not in my budget."

"Life's short," I heard him saying. Perhaps his experience—

dying at the age of seventy-seven—was now altering his views of frivolity and finance.

In an email I wrote to Barry, I said, "You may be wondering why I haven't been in lately. Tommy died November 2, and it's been too painful to return. But my seventy-fifth birthday is coming up, and in honor of that occasion, and in memory of Tommy, would you consider opening on a Monday night for a private party?"

Five days before my actual birthday, on a Monday when the restaurant doors bore taped signs that read PRIVATE PARTY, I stood with a friend who had clasped me in a hug. "It's a shame Tommy couldn't be here," she said.

I smiled, stepped back, and surveyed the happy crowd. Above the cheery noise of forty friends and relatives, and with Barry on hand to supervise the celebration, I shouted to be heard. "Oh, he's here. He's definitely here. In fact, he threw it for me."

Fifty-Nine:
Homeward Bound

The first thing I saw was an American flag flying from a pole attached to the roof of the porch. My heart lifted. It wasn't patriotism that buoyed my spirits, but a sign that the new owners of our old house had changed its appearance.

I had dreaded returning to the place where Tommy and I, and our golden retriever Buddy, had lived for thirteen years. Because my departure was spurred not by happy events but by my husband's death, this visit was stained with sadness.

When I first received the invitation to share the graduation celebration for a former neighbor's children, I told my daughter, "I don't think I can go. The party house is right across from ours. It will be too painful."

As I spoke those words, I envisioned our blue-trimmed house with porch steps that needed painting, the flowerpots that Tommy hung each summer, and the decorative bench that sat along one side.

I conjured images of Buddy and me seated on the top step. When my picture included my husband on his red Schwinn, rounding the corner heading toward our house, I couldn't stop the tears.

"Do you have to go?" my daughter asked. "I'm sure they'll understand."

"I love the graduates, and I believe they'd like me to be there," I said. "Maybe I have to think of them instead of me."

On the day of the graduation party, I rode the familiar Blue Line train to my stop. The cars were filled with passengers and luggage on the way to the final destination of O'Hare Airport. Going home, I thought to myself that these travelers were likely looking forward to their return, while I was worried about my reaction.

I could have walked on the opposite side of the street, but was drawn toward my old house, where the sight of the flag eased my passage. When I arrived at my address, a large black dog raced down the steps to greet me. "Sorry," said someone on the porch, as he tried to move the dog, which was now happily being petted.

"No, it's okay," I said. "I love dogs. This used to be my house."

He reached out a hand. "Hi, I'm a brother-in-law. Let me get the owners."

When he went inside to retrieve them, I introduced myself to people sitting on the porch. My apprehension began evaporating as I witnessed how much others were appreciating this beloved spot.

A couple, likely in their forties, were exuberant in their greetings. "We've heard so much about you from the neighbors. We're happy to finally meet you. Would you like to come inside?"

I hesitated. I was doing okay so far, hadn't fallen apart, but could the interior send me over the edge? "Have you changed the inside?" I asked. "If it looks different, I think I can handle it."

"Come in," they said. They led me inside and were as tender as if I were returning to a long-ago childhood home, rather than one left a mere four months ago.

Several of the former white living room walls were painted bright colors. The wooden floors had been finished in a darker stain. The stair banisters were now white. In the kitchen, the oak cabinets had also been painted white.

I couldn't recognize this house! There was no repetition of the many pieces of art we had hung on our white walls. A large sectional had replaced the facing couches that had cushioned Tommy and Buddy on one and me on the other.

"Do you want to see upstairs?" they asked.

I was growing confident. "Sure," I said. More painted walls; a crib in the smallest bedroom; an alcove there, once stuffed with extra bedding, had become a closet for baby clothes; new carpeting in all of the bedrooms. I was as delighted as if I had been the contractor who had performed the renovations.

I cooed at and praised the remake, not so much because I admired their decorating choices but because everything looked completely different.

We shook hands when I left. "I know you'll enjoy the house and the neighbors as much as we did," I said.

"We love it already," they said.

The party was sweet; the neighbors were grateful I had attended. When I left, as I walked back to the Blue Line on the opposite side of the street of my old house, I stopped for a final look.

"Good-bye," I said, with just a slight mist blurring my vision. I put two fingers to my lips and blew my old house a kiss. Then I continued my journey home.

Sixty:
California Dreaming

"How often do you get to see your parents?" I asked the limo driver.

"Only every few years," he said.

We were in bumper-to-bumper traffic en route to LAX, where a flight would return me home to Chicago. I had started this query as a diversion, and because of an itch I had packed along with the contents of my suitcase.

"How do you feel about that schedule? Does it work well for everyone in your family?" I was settling into the smooth black leather seats of the luxury car, and grateful for the driver's willingness to share.

"I don't like it," he said. "I wish they lived here full-time. They're getting older—my father had small strokes a few months ago, and it would've taken me ten hours to get to Peru."

I hadn't thought about that, about an adult child's reasoning for wanting his older parents to live closer. Could it be that part of my California daughter's wish to have me live in her city was partially based on this concern?

The possibility of a move started as a seasonal idea. "Maybe I'll come in February and, instead of staying my usual four days, I'll spend a few weeks," I said. "Get away from Chicago's winter."

"Listen, Mom," she said. "You may not believe me, but when I told you I'd love you to move here, I meant every word of it."

"Well, if I ever did move there, I wouldn't want to live with

169

you. I wouldn't want to be sitting around waiting for you to escort me somewhere."

"Who said you could live with me?" She was joking; I was sure of it.

"Maybe I could rent a small apartment? And a car?" As we talked, I could feel the discussion moving from italics to bold. Was I considering a sunbird's getaway, or something more permanent?

By now, I was playing my own devil's advocate. "Actually, with Tommy and Buddy gone, there's really nothing to hold me in Chicago," I said. "I got rid of most of my possessions when I moved to my rental. It'd be one load for a cross-country moving truck."

"Oh, oh," said my other daughter, in earshot. "If Mom's thinking about it, it'll happen."

"No, no," I said. "I haven't decided anything. We're just talking here. But it would be nice to see my grandchildren grow up. And maybe with me here, you'd move, too?"

"I have a life in Boston," she said. "But it would be great to have you and Sis in the same place."

The discussion ended at that spot but continued to swirl around on my ride out of Los Angeles, on my plane, and when I landed at O'Hare.

"Good to be home" were my first words as I settled into the cab that would take me to my apartment in River North. *"Home"— where did that come from?* What had happened to my temptation to move to California?

My sentimental feelings about the city where I was born and had lived nearly my entire life continued as I entered my building's lobby.

"Welcome home!" said the evening concierge. There was that word, "home," again. Was he somehow privy to the back-and-forth going on in my head?

And when I unlocked the door to my apartment, my declaration "I'm home" was automatically shouted out.

I dropped my luggage and cozied into the couch to survey my doll-size estate. Paintings on every wall, our wedding photo and pictures of our dogs arrayed on a built-in bookshelf, my small office desk and bench, floor-to-ceiling windows with their awesome display of the river and nightscape—all exuded a warm familiarity. "I love you!" I blurted out.

That's when I realized how much I had come to adore my new place, which had quickly become a refuge and cocoon cushioning me from the sad events that propelled me to this new life. How could I ever leave this solace?

How could I leave a friend I've cleaved to since sixth-grade grammar school, to dozens more friends won over the years, to treasured relatives?

And how could I leave a recently joined Chicago Sinai Congregation study group that was helping me refresh my spiritual self?

The path was clear: If concern for my health is a factor, I'll assure my faraway daughters that my strong support group will be at the ready in case of a medical emergency; no need to immediately hop a plane to be at my bedside.

Then I'll book one week—two weeks, tops—in LA in February. Afterward, I'll return home, to Chicago, where I belong, and where I'll continue my new, independent, nourishing life.

Sixty-One:
Forget Him Not

"Please forgive me, honey," I said.

Tommy was ignoring me and was instead stepping up to a teed ball.

"I don't know how it happened," I continued. "I wrote August 24 in ink on my paper calendar and entered the date on my Apple and Google calendars. But when it arrived—maybe because it was a Saturday—your birthday simply slipped away."

This attempt at an Earth-to-heaven conversation was taking place in bed. The August lapse had hit me upon awakening. For this supplication, I was propped up on pillows, where on one side were views of morning light edging up my windows, and on the other were framed photographs of my husband.

With guilt covering me like the nearby blanket, I chose to focus not on his portrait but on the scene I was conjuring in my head. So far, it was not going as anticipated.

Still ignoring me, my husband raised his club and, as I'd seen him do hundred of times, slammed the golf ball, then returned to his stance to watch it sail across the green.

"Gorgeous!" I said, hoping my praise would swing his attention to me.

I chose a golf course for my apology scene because that's where Tommy spent so many happy hours. I figured in that setting, he'd be in a mood to forgive his wife.

Maybe he's snubbing me, I thought. Birthdays were never a

big deal to him. In our fourteen years of marriage, my husband refused offers of parties, preferring dinners out with close friends.

And when I'd plead for clues for his present, he'd shrug and say, "You don't have to get me anything." Of course, I'd ignore that response, and, along with a chocolate cake, awaiting his awakening on his birthday morning would be a wrapped mystery novel, or a dozen golf balls, or a dressy shirt I'd have to remind him to wear.

Lacking a reaction, I continued pressing my regrets because the incident frightened me. It wasn't that I worried about frays in my memory; it was the nag that if I forgot Tommy's birthday, did that mean I was forgetting him?

I had been certain my nightly routine would seal my husband in my brain. "You'll be happy to hear I did thirty minutes on the bike," I'll tell him. "Good girl!" he'll say from the fancy gym I place him in.

As with the golf course, I frequently set Tommy in a tableau I know he'll enjoy. I visualize my three-times-a-week YMCA athlete now ensconced in a workout area favored by world-class athletes. I see Babe Ruth, Johnny Weissmuller, Walter Payton, and Bobby Jones mingling with my guy.

In this setting, he's happy to see me. I wait until my strongman finishes bench pressing and wipes down the equipment with a paper towel. I watch wistfully as his body, shiny with sweat, takes a drink from his favorite water bottle.

But in this morning's heart-to-heart, it appears I haven't yet convinced my husband of my repentance. So I try a more spiritual tack. Although he wasn't Jewish, Tommy was the one who encouraged me to light Sabbath candles. "*Shabbat shalom*," he'd energetically respond when I completed the ritual.

"You know Friday night is the beginning of Yom Kippur," I said. "Before that day, I must seek reconciliation for the wrongs committed against others. You're at the top of my list.

"And, to make sure it doesn't happen again, I've got a reminder set on the 2014 Jewish calendar. There, honey, your Hebrew birthday is August 22. Like you've seen me do with my parents', I'll light a *yahrzeit* candle in your memory. That'll give me two days before your actual birthday to catch the date. Will you forgive me now?"

Finally, Tommy paused at the next hole. He leaned over to place a golf ball on a tee, then stood straight up and faced me. He was smiling, with brown eyes as sunny as I remembered them. "Of course I forgive you, sweetheart," he said. "You know I could never stay mad at you. Now scram—you're holding up the foursome behind us."

Sixty-Two:
I'll Call You

He was sitting in a chair, a metal walker at his side. Slightly bent over, he smiled at each person who entered the house.

"You look familiar," he said as I neared his post. He tilted his head as if a new position would bring me into sharper focus.

"I'm a friend of Leah's," I said. "We met several times at her house."

"Sit down and talk to me," he said. "I'm a friendly guy."

It was Saturday night, a holiday party at the home of friends. The place was crowded with people of varying ages. Some were lining up at the buffet that held deli trays; others had already piled their paper plates and were seated at a long table.

I took a seat on the cushioned arm of a couch next to him.

"What's this song?" he said. "They sparkle, they bubble . . . "

"'Them There Eyes,'" I said.

"Right! 'Them There Eyes'!" He looked at me admiringly, as if I were a successful game-show contestant.

"So, listen," he said, "I just got an iPad, and I'm enjoying the heck out of it."

"That's great," I said. "Do you read books on it?"

"No, no, I just talk to my grandkids. I like the feel of real books. I'm reading *The Jewish Police*," he said. "I love it. It's by . . . It's by . . . "

"*The Yiddish Policemen's Union*," I said. "By Michael Chabon. I have it on my iPad."

"Yeah," he said. "Michael Chabon. How did you know that?"

"I read a lot," I said. "Books, newspapers. I keep up with pop culture."

"Michael Chabon," he repeated. It seemed like he had been Scotch-taping his memory and the notion that someone near his age had pulled an author's name out of a hat was astonishing.

"Can I have your phone number?" he said. "Maybe we could have coffee or something. You're so literate."

Then he added what he must've believed were the magic words that would make any single older woman swoon: "I drive."

I looked at the walker at his side. He saw my glance. "It's because of my arthritis. But I can still drive."

"You don't remember," I said. "We went on a date after my divorce from my first husband. Leah fixed us up."

He looked at me, perhaps trying to scoop through and find my twenty-years-younger version. "Sorry, I don't remember. Did we have a good time?"

I could see that date perfectly. Jeffrey and I met at a coffee house in Wicker Park. We sat on the patio. I wore tight jeans, a patterned silk blouse, and high-heeled boots. I looked sharp.

He was a dentist, intelligent. Up on politics and other topics we shared. I recall he was nice looking and full of himself and had not a whit of interest in me. He never called after that first date.

This night, at the party, I wrote my phone number on a card and handed it to him. "Maybe we can meet next week," he said.

"No," I said. "My daughters are coming into town. I'll be busy all week." This was a partial lie. They weren't arriving until Friday. There were five days when a coffee date could've fit in. But I was backing away from a tangle I didn't want to set foot in. Tommy hadn't been gone a year; I was skittish about dating.

"Okay," he said.

I left to mingle. When I found Leah, I whispered in her ear, "Jeffrey asked for my phone number."

My friend looked at me as if I had just revealed I'd decided to take up skydiving. "No, no," she said. "He's bad news. Don't get involved with him."

"I didn't know what to do," I said. "He said I was literate. He said he drives." We chuckled at his prideful asset.

"Promise me you won't go out with him," she said.

"I promise."

The next morning, a Sunday, Jeffrey called. "Remember, I said I'd call to make a coffee date."

"My kids are coming to town," I said, repeating the excuse I had offered less than twenty-four hours earlier. "Not this week. I'll call you."

I dialed Leah's number. "Jeffrey called. I didn't know what to do, so I said I'd call him back."

"Don't!" she said. "Did you see the shape he's in? What do you need that for? On top of that, he's got a temper. You know I love you and want you to one day find a boyfriend, but promise me you'll stay away from him."

"Not a problem," I said. "I just won't return his call. He forgot meeting me twenty years ago; maybe he'll even forget he asked for my number last night."

Sixty-Three:
Déjà Vu

I watch as the nurse places two plastic bags in the locker. One holds my friend's shoes; the other, clothing he has removed following the nurse's instructions.

"Will my stuff be safe?" he says to me.

"If you like, I'll put your wallet and watch in my tote," I say.

What I don't tell my longtime friend, whom I've accompanied to this outpatient ambulatory surgical center, is that I've got this down pat. In Tommy's case, I stowed his aged wallet and wristwatch in my bag, which they never left until I placed them on a mini-memorial atop his chest of drawers in our bedroom.

"I left my wallet at home," my friend says.

"So, no worry," I say. I sit on a chair facing his bed while we wait for another nurse to come in to get his vitals. Next, the anesthesiologist reviews drugs they will use to knock him out, and finally the surgeon appears to discuss what happens next.

While this is going on, I zone out and recall the time a year ago when I sat with Tommy in a pre-op area. As I wrote in an early chapter the ENT team had planned to insert a feeding tube down his throat so he could get nourishment. He was dehydrated—that's what brought us initially to the hospital— and the tube was to solve his problem. Then we'd be on our way home.

After they wheeled Tommy out of the pre-op area to perform the procedure, I returned to his hospital room. The phone rang.

"We have a problem," said the doctor on the other end. "When we tried to insert the tube, there was a blockage. We're pretty sure it's cancer."

The voice of my friend's surgeon wakes me: "He'll be out of surgery in a half hour, so just stay put in the waiting area."

Sure enough, before I know it, the surgeon finds me to say, "He did great. You can go in and see him." My friend looks fine and is chatty. Perhaps the painkillers, or his relief that all is over, is making him eager to converse.

But as we talk, this latest nurse is monitoring his blood pressure, and it is too high. Could our gabbing be the culprit?

"Do you mind?" my friend asks, with an eye to the closed curtain that will lead me out.

"No problem," I say. Then, once more, I go to thoughts of Tommy and the time he was in this hospital and wouldn't let me out of his sight. During the ten days he was here, I slept on a cushioned window seat. On the few nights I didn't stay over, I'd return to find him wearing a weighted vest.

"He tried to leave," a nurse explained. "Had his clothing, shoes, and baseball cap on. Was halfway down the hall before we caught him." Often I'd wish he had escaped, for those hospital days were the worst of my life—heartbreaking and fruitless.

Once my friend's blood pressure subsides, I'm allowed to return to his room. He is dressed and ready to be escorted via a wheelchair to the curb, where a cab will return us to his nearby apartment.

At his high-rise, I push open the lobby doors to save him from exertion. We go upstairs, and I hang out for a few hours, until I'm satisfied he can be on his own. "I can call neighbors if I have problems," he says. "Go home."

When my Tommy was finally released from the hospital—on his internists' advice to forgo risky surgery because it would be torturous and not cure his aphasia or his increasing dementia—it was an ambulance that took us home.

When we arrived, neighbors were waiting. I stood on the porch as the drivers lifted his stretcher up the stairs. The neighbors followed and held the front door open. With a gentleness and reverence that reminded me of a potentate's litter, our caravan moved to our bedroom, where a hospital bed awaited.

With Tommy safely settled in the house where we lived for thirteen years, away from the hospital setting I had grown to despise, the neighbors stayed to help set up the equipment. Oxygen tanks and medical supplies stuffed the room.

An evening phone call to my postsurgery friend confirms he is managing okay. The painkillers are doing their job, and he is comfortable watching television. "Thanks for being there for me," he says.

Because Tommy wasn't able to speak for the last year of his life, I didn't get those same words. But, as many a caregiver will tell you, it was an honor to be there for him.

Sixty-Four:
Jealousy at the Gym

"I thought you said you'd never get married again." It is my deceased husband, Tommy, who startles me awake.

"Where did you get the idea I'm getting married?" I say. His voice, which started in a dream, has shifted me from prone to upright in bed.

"I saw you at the health club. Heard your conversation with your trainer, Kim. You were asking her to introduce you to some guy."

"I thought you hated the East Bank Club," I said, referring to the posh fitness place I'd tried to get Tommy to join. "What were you doing there?"

"Keeping an eye on you," he said.

"Look," I said. "I'm still wearing my wedding ring, and I have no intention of ever taking it off." I raised my left hand to the ceiling, assuming the image could break through the stucco and reach my complaining husband.

As I waited for his response, I thought back to the day in 1998 when he and I walked across Ashland Avenue to Service Merchandise, where we purchased our $25 gold bands. After our wedding in Las Vegas, where we placed them on each other's finger under the guidance of an ecumenical minister and sixteen guests, I never took the ring off.

"Listen, Tommy," I said. "I don't ever want to marry again. You are my last husband. But would you mind if I started to date?

It's been nearly a year, and I'm beginning to feel the need for a male companion. I miss the 'What did you do today?' conversations and a guy on my arm."

There was silence from my celestial spouse. Although in the last years of his life I had become accustomed to his aphasia, in our imaginary conversations, I had returned him to full voice. That's why this pause bothered me. Was he angry and retreating from our beloved dialogues, or was he contemplating my question?

"You change your mind so much," he said, ignoring my excuse.

"I won't debate that," I said, counting on my easy agreement to let me off the hook.

"I heard you tell your daughters and your friends you were glad you rented a small apartment because there'd be no room for anyone else in it. Did you mean that?"

"True," I said. "But I'm talking about *dating* someone, not having him move in with me."

"Well, it was hard for me to hear you asking your trainer to play Cupid," Tommy said. "You can understand that."

"Of course I do, honey," I said. "But I'm spending too many nights at home—me and TV. When you were alive and we watched shows together, that was one thing. But I've continued our tradition in spades. Now, with Apple TV and Netflix, I'm more tied to the set than ever."

"What's wrong with that?" he asked.

I smiled as I recalled our evenings on our two couches, each of us stretched out, watching our favorite shows night after night.

"No, honey, you're right," I said. "I loved every minute of our marriage. And I know I'll never find another guy who wants to sit home and watch TV with me."

"Well, it seems like you're trying hard to replace me," he said. "I also heard you asking your two lawyer friends to keep an eye out for a single man your age."

Now I was rankled. Tommy had disdained my health club in favor of his plain YMCA. Oh, he liked the golf center all right, and he enjoyed running its track on winter days. But when I posited joint membership, he turned up his nose. Now it appeared I couldn't get him away from the place.

"Okay, you're right," I said. "I did ask Jimmy and John to keep me in mind. I've known both of them for years, and they're my same age. I thought they'd be good matchmakers."

"They're both Jewish, aren't they? Is that what you're looking for? Finished with Gentiles, are you?"

"No, no, honey," I said. "I didn't specify a religion. In fact, I wouldn't mind someone who's not Jewish. You and I were in tune despite our different faiths."

Another pause from above. Had I convinced Tommy of my innocent need for a companion and not a husband? Had he retreated to his heavenly home, contented he would never be replaced?

Then came that voice, which I can still hear clearly. "Listen, sweetheart, I'm really just teasing you. It makes me happy to hear you're thinking about dating. That means you haven't soured on men, that my part in your life has you seeking another me."

"Never another you," I said.

Sixty-Five:
From Third Wheel to Driver's Seat

As I skipped from table to table at the bar mitzvah luncheon, I felt a novel emotion. Although I wasn't paired up like my friends who were attending the same celebration, I lacked any sense of third wheel–ness.

I felt no envy, no mad desire to be coupled—simply a feeling of being comfortable enough to chat with strangers who were seat companions or in the buffet line, and anyone who caught my interest.

This was a very different experience than my previous episode of singleness. After my divorce from my first husband and before my marriage to Tommy, I relished my freedom for a bit but then wanted desperately to be paired up. I hated being the gal left at the ballroom table to keep an eye on purses while couples danced. I yearned for a man on my arm so I would better fit in with my married friends.

The *Chicago Reader* was the Match.com of its day, and I found several men there to date. In the auditions, I was impartial. Fellows whom I would've ignored if I hadn't been so nauseatingly needy would get at least one date.

Of course, that was twenty-three years ago and I have grown up since then. And although I have, on these pages, admitted to eyeing men at the gym, I just don't have the same pathetic ache, which I attribute to several factors:

I really enjoy the studio apartment I have chosen to replace our home. Although it's only 615 square feet, at my petite size, it feels like a perfect fit. There is no space for a roommate and his stuff.

At bedtime, I use a pillow as a stand-in for my late husband. In spoon position, I tell him my day's activities. While this lacks an audible response from my proxy, I can easily imagine his voice and sweet good night. Schmaltzy as this sounds, it totally lulls me to sleep.

At the luncheon I described in the opening paragraph of this chapter, I witnessed several friends who either were full-blown caretakers of their spouses or were struggling with the impending role. Their plights reminded me of the last years of Tommy's life, when I was an around-the-clock caregiver. I have to selfishly admit, I am not eager to reenlist for the job, which, at my age, is a real possibility.

Except for a few longtime friends, most of my crowd is single. If I want companionship, a phone call, email, or text message can usually find me a delightful sidekick. And this pal is likely to be agreeable to my choice of event or menu.

Although I no longer own a car, I have learned how to travel throughout the city and suburbs via public transportation. For example, here's how I got to the aforementioned Skokie bar mitzvah: I caught the Brown Line at the Merchandise Mart, exited at Kedzie, took the 93 Foster bus to Dempster, and then took the 250 Pace bus to Central Park. Okay, it was ninety minutes door to door, but I had a window seat and a scenic adventure.

My waking and sleeping schedule would likely deter any potential swain. And I'm reluctant to adjust my body clock just to be part of a couple. I suspect that a single man seeking a girlfriend would want his female companion to remain awake throughout a movie or play, erect on a dance floor, and conscious for a goodnight kiss.

I love television. No, I mean I *really love* television. My favorite evening activity—prior to falling asleep on the couch—is to watch preferred episodes on HBO, Showtime, or Netflix. This viewing is typically accompanied by feet propped on my coffee table, an ice-cream dish in my paws, and a sigh of solo satisfaction. Would a suitor find this alluring? Would I be forced to share my Edy's Slow Churned Butter Pecan?

I won't change my appearance or wardrobe to hook a guy. In my earlier single stage, I wore three-inch heels and clothing I deemed alluring, and shopped at Victoria's Secret for "just in case" dates. Now, I refuse to dye my gray hair, get Botox or plastic surgery, or don anything that doesn't stretch.

Having said all of the above, I will add that if you, dear reader, were to identify a divorced or widowed male in my age group who still drives—better yet, at night—I might be persuaded to shift some of my reasoning. For there *are* times when a ride in the passenger seat, with a sweet, bright, funny guy at the wheel, does sound tempting.

Sixty-Six:
A Resting Place in the Garden of Eden

"Be sure you blow out the candle before you go to bed." It was my husband's voice reaching out to me. This was a familiar warning, because when Tommy was alive, he repeated that order every Friday night after I lit the Shabbat candles.

"It has to stay on for twenty-four hours," I said, not aloud, just in my head, as I have done in many of our afterlife conversations. "It's a memorial candle; it marks your November 2 anniversary."

"Your people are weird," Tommy said. "Why celebrate my death? Why not my birthday? Our marriage?"

"It's not a celebration," I said. "More an occasion to remember our loved ones. Did you hear me recite the memorial prayer 'His resting place shall be in the Garden of Eden'? I like that. It helps me cope."

I went on, "I imagine you in my version of the Garden of Eden, playing golf with Bill and some other departed duffers. Your voice is fully repaired, so you're teasing each other with each shot. Am I close?"

"Pretty good," Tommy said. "Add in that we never have to reserve a tee time. We can walk on any course, any time of day or night."

I loved that image, so I took our conversation a step further. "Can you believe, sweetheart, it's been an entire year? Blink of an eye," I said.

"Well, you've been a busy girl during that year."

In my mind, his voice was proud, not angry. I recognized that cherished tone because it was one that bound me so closely to this second mate. I could see him at the 2006 book launch for my memoir—first row, first seat—beaming at me as I stood on the stage of Women and Children First.

Tommy was my first reader for the book. I'd hand him ten pages, which he'd grab as eagerly as if I were writing one of the Elmore Leonard or Ruth Rendell novels he loved.

"Great," he'd say. Or sometimes, "I don't like the chapter title" or, "I don't understand this Yiddish word." Those reviews were my cue to alter or translate.

"Yes, it has been quite a year," I said, winding back to his assessment. "You supported all of my activities, right, honey?"

There was a hush from my elusive conversation partner. *He's likely reminiscing about our house*, I thought, *the one we lived in happily with Buddy. The house I sold.*

A few beats later, his response: "It was hard to watch you leave Dakin Street," he said, confirming my suspicion. "But I understood you had no choice. Without me to do the maintenance stuff and without Buddy to protect you, it was too large and too risky to stay alone. Still, I felt a pang."

I quickly changed the subject, which was raw for both of us. "So, Tommy," I said, "how are you keep tabs on me? Watching on high from a cloud?"

"I read your blogs," he said.

I hit pause on our chat as I quickly reviewed a year's worth of posts. Had they all been favorable? Had I exposed anything he would prefer hidden?

When I started the first blog, *The Rookie Caregiver*, I called him to my computer and asked if he'd like to read what I had written.

"Pull up a chair," I said, nervous about his reaction. My husband was more private than I, even cagey about his past, so I worried how he would feel about this Internet publicity.

But he avoided a seat and instead stood behind me as I scrolled through the pages. He patted my shoulder, and raised two thumbs, his universal sign back then of "okay by me."

"You're fine with all of this past year's posts?" I said to my dearly departed. I wanted to be sure I understood him correctly. I knew there could be several filters between heaven and Earth that might mess with communication.

"Sure," he said. "I'm quite the superstar up here. Everyone is jealous they're not kept alive—well, sort of—like I am."

"Your privacy," I said. "You don't have a problem with me sharing our stories with the world?"

"Sweetheart, don't get a big head. It's *your* world, *your* friends, and *your* fans. You've never kept secrets from them."

I was relieved to hear this, to get Tommy's blessing. "Okay, honey," I said. "You can rest easy. I promise to blow out the candle before I go to bed."

"Good girl," he said; then, "Love you, Wifey."

"Love you, too, Hubber," I said, misting at the memory of our pet names for each other.

Sixty-Seven:
Double-Dating with My Mother

I could chalk it up to the difficulty older Jewish men have when they try to navigate technology. Or I can just admit I'm a loser on JDate. My evidence: although I've "favorited" sixteen matches, zero have returned the compliment.

"I thought you weren't interested in meeting men." It was my deceased mother, elbowing herself past Tommy into my subconscious.

Her arrival was hardly a surprise. After all, rather than my late husband being invested in finding me a date, it was more likely to be my mother, Min, a beauty who died at the age of sixty-seven.

"Mom," I said to the apparition pulling up a chair next to me, "I don't want anyone moving in, but I think I'd enjoy dinner or a play with a nice guy my age."

"Well, I can tell you what your problem is," she said. "Your profile isn't sexy enough."

"Sexy isn't me. I'm trying to be honest."

"Honest—ha!" she said. "I see you've put your age at seventy. Remember, I was present at your birth, and you're off by five years."

"No one admits their real age in online dating," I said. "I recall you telling me more than once you never wanted to get old."

In my mind's eye, I could see my mother hesitate before responding. She was using her right hand to sweep her hairdo upward and a mirror to be certain her eye shadow, mascara, and red lipstick were in place.

"Well, if I had known what good shape a woman could be in her seventies, I might have stuck around. I have to admit, you've kept your weight down."

A compliment from my mother! I preened in my office chair and brushed aside childhood memories of her fixated on my chubbiness, rather than my brain.

"I see two matches answered your emails," she went on. "It's a shame you had to make the first move."

Ah, here's the familiar motherly dig. "That's not a problem for me, Mom, being aggressive. That's how I landed Tommy. I asked him out for our first date."

There was silence on the other end of our celestial chat. Although she died before Tommy and I met and married, I knew Mom would have had mixed feelings about my second husband. It wasn't the fact that he wasn't Jewish; it was that he wasn't rich.

"Don't blame your mother for wanting an easier life for her daughter," she said, evidently overhearing my thoughts. "But I did appreciate how much he loved you."

I didn't want to bring Tommy into this scenario, so I quickly returned to my failure on JDate. "Did you notice, Mom, that no matter their age, all of my matches wanted someone between fifty and sixty-five?"

"So," she said, stretching out the vowel, "you couldn't have dropped ten years?"

I sighed. "Mom, that's just not me. I've come a long way, and I'm proud of the woman I've become. I'm not that desperate to make myself over for some dude."

Now, a sigh from Min. "So, try it your way. Be honest. Don't say you're passionate, fun, adventurous in the bedroom."

I laughed. "So you've been reading my competition."

"Of course—it can get boring up here. It's a change of pace to read fantasies about ideal matches. My girlfriends and I had a good laugh."

"Were you laughing when one of the guys answered my email with the news he had already fallen in love with the second woman he met on JDate?" I said.

"See, you didn't move fast enough. You have to jump in as soon as you find someone interesting."

"I don't know, Mom. Did you also read that he is now spending all of his time with his new romance?"

"So, what's the problem?"

"I gagged when I saw that. I don't want anyone spending all of his time with me; it's suffocating. Like I said, dinner out, a movie, a play, that's all I'm thinking about, not him taking over my life."

"So, have it your way," she said. "I assume, with your record of zero and sixteen, you're bowing out. No more online dating?"

"Not completely," I said. "It is kind of a fun game, and my ego is strong enough to take the rejections. So next month, I'm going to the other side."

"Women!" she said. "Don't tell me you're going to become a lesbian."

"No, Mom, Match dot com. I'm going to check out the Gentiles. Maybe they'll be more open to an adorable, gray-haired woman in her midseventies."

"Try sixty-five, and you may have a shot," she said.

Sixty-Eight:
Offended 2013

If a guy told you his three grown sons have refused to speak to him for twenty years, or that the wife he divorced is as silent as their kids, wouldn't your first question be, *Another woman?*

No? Then obviously you are not as nosy as I, or are not the investigative-reporter type.

My query occurred during a JDate phone conversation. (I realize that on these pages I claimed I was dropping the Jewish online-dating site, but I decided to give it one more month.) He—let's call him by a new screen name, Offended2013—had given me his phone number and recommended that I block my own cell number. This was a point in his favor, I thought—a gentleman.

According to my iPhone, we talked for fifty-eight minutes. During that time, I learned we had some things in common: we both lived in the city, we were around the same age (he claimed seventy-one; I fudged seventy), we enjoyed plays, and we had Spain and Greece on our travel wish list. Our differences—he was not a TV addict like I am, he liked being out frequently in the evenings—might've been possible for me to overcome.

Before our conversation ended, we made plans to meet for coffee. But the following morning, I received this message from Offended2013:

"i am cancelling our meeting wed. i really was hurt and offended by your quick remark about my devorce having to do with another woman. i felt you were out of line. that was not the case. i just didnt appreciate it. that is far from the type of person i am."

"I apologize," I wrote in a message back to him. "It's your call. Good luck with your search." But he blocked any further correspondence from me, so my attempt to backpedal is floating somewhere in cyberspace.

Daughter Faith (yes, I had to share) responded, "I am offended he does not know how to spell 'divorce.'" From Jill: "The atrocious spelling is enough for you to block him forever."

Perhaps it was wrong of me to jump to the conclusion I conjured, but I speak from experience: my first husband, of thirty years, left me for another woman.

Our clichéd drama began when I noticed he was looking exceptionally fit and well dressed. "I think he's having an affair," I said to my best friend, Judy.

"Don't ask him if he's having an affair," she said. "Just say, 'I know you're having an affair.'"

I'll never forget that prophetic conversation, which took place in 1990, during one of our regular Saturday lunches at the Bon Ton restaurant on Chicago's Gold Coast. As Judy and I munched our poached-chicken sandwiches, we kept our voices low because adjacent diners seemed to be leaning our way.

A few days after my friend's counsel, I put the phrase to use. I had been asleep in our king-size bed when the phone rang. Because my husband's profession often brought emergency requests, I knew the call would be for him. "The phone's ringing," I said, as I rolled over to rouse him. But there was an empty space where he usually slept.

I went downstairs, dumped myself on the couch, and waited. "What are you doing up?" he asked as he entered through the back door. He appeared to be playing a soap opera part. If he hadn't spotted me, he surely would've been toting his oxfords and tiptoeing in on stocking feet.

Then came my line: "I know you're having an affair."

"How did you know?"

"Your new clothes, your slimmer body, your indifference to me and the kids."

He sank down next to me on the couch. We both cried. (What can I say? I'm not the pottery-slinging type, and I held some responsibility for a marriage gone sour.) "Will you come with me to a marriage counselor?" I asked.

We had one session. The morning after, he descended the stairs with a gym bag in his hand. "I'm checking into a hotel; I'll call you later." He was glum; I was, I must admit, relieved, and grateful to the other woman for handing him the bad-guy role and me the sympathetic character.

Fortunately, in the intervening twenty-three-plus years, my ex and I have remained good friends. He is my emergency contact, and I am his companion for doctor visits.

So, with this history, I stand firm in defense of my question. Now I think Offended2013 doth protest too much. If not another woman, then what?

Sixty-Nine:
Ink Fades, but Memories Linger

"Cool."

I glanced at my left bicep to follow the pointing hand of a trainer at my health club.

"Oh, you mean my tattoo?"

"Yeah. What does it say?"

I stretched my neck and pulled my arm closer to read it for him. But as I searched for the words, I made an unhappy discovery. "It's faded," I said. How had I not noticed that before? "I guess I shouldn't have been surprised; it had been inked fifteen years earlier, for my sixtieth birthday.

"Wow," he said. Was he doing the math or wondering why a sixty-year-old would've gotten her first-time tattoo at that age?

Our chat inspired me to cut my exercise routine and revisit the occasion of my tattoo. I stretched out on a bench, and it all came back.

When that birthday was nearing, friends and loved ones queried, "How do you plan to celebrate?" Expecting news of a gala party, a European trip, or expensive jewelry, they learned instead, "I'm getting a tattoo."

"Are you nuts?" my brother, Ron, asked. "When I was in the army, any woman with a tattoo was considered a hooker."

Husband Tommy's response was gentler: "It's not my arm, but if that's what you want, go ahead."

Daughters Faith and Jill, a musician and a writer, predictably pronounced the plan "terrific."

The next question was: "Why?" To me, achieving age sixty was a chance to thumb my nose at society, a don't-give-a-damn-what-anyone-thinks time to stray from conformity. So there'll be critics—who cares? After many in my age group have endured the collapse of a long marriage, kids who grow up and leave, and loved ones who die too soon, we get our priorities straight, and a barb tossed our way is harmless.

Deciding on a design was difficult, considering it would be my companion till dust do us part. Finally, I settled on a tattoo with a heart that would contain two banners, each bearing a daughter's name. And it would be a joyful artwork, a tribute to my talented daughters, honoring them for our solid relationship and their own free spirits.

Finding my tattoo artist was easier. From referrals, I settled on Jon. He was in his late thirties, slightly built, perhaps five foot eight, small beard, earrings, and colorful tattoos slithering down each arm. He lifted pant legs and shirt to reveal even more images.

"It must be fun, carnival-like," I instructed, "with symbols of my daughters' personalities." He quickly sketched a chubby heart, musical notes, rays of sun, and roses emanating from all sides. Across the center were two banners: FAITH, the eldest, on the upper; JILL, eighteen months younger, on the lower. It was perfect. In one week, the design would be ready for application.

The second appointment produced the finished product on translucent paper: my puffy heart, in psychedelic colors of crimson, yellow, turquoise, and emerald, with my daughters' names emblazoned on its front. "Let's do it!" I said.

Jon perched me on a high stool and gently placed my left arm on his worktable, where lay brand-new needles wrapped in sterile paper, a palette of glistening pigments in individual pots, antiseptic liquids, cotton, and other reassuring paraphernalia.

I looked away as Jon applied the needle, but honestly it didn't hurt. The sensation was more of a pressurized tickle, accompanied by a low buzz. The whole operation was soothing, as if I were at the beauty salon for my customary shampoo and cut.

After two hours, the tattoo was complete. I was alive—no blood, no pain, just a sensation like a sunburn. I stared into the mirror, praying for satisfaction, and saw my badge of courage: a wildly colored tattoo, four and three-quarters inches wide by three inches high, with my cherished daughters' names forever engraved on my arm.

At home that afternoon, Tommy was eager to view the results, but I pleaded, "Wait till morning," preferring to keep my raw portrait protected in its plastic bunting.

I couldn't sleep at all that night. Visions of regrets, onlookers' gasps, and lifelong pain prohibited repose. I prayed for the hours to race by. In the morning, I ran to the bathroom and was ecstatic to find my gorgeous tattoo intact. It was bright, fun, and, well, tough!

Today, with Tommy gone, but still brighter in my memory than my fading tattoo, I recall his response: "I love it!" he said. "It's sexy."

Rather than refreshing the ink on my fifteen-year-old tattoo, as I first considered, I think I'll leave it as is. Somehow, the soft colors seem more appropriate for a widow. But who knows how I'll feel at eighty—perhaps a brand-new one?

Seventy:
To Be Adored

I winced at my dear friend's words. "Why in the world would you want ANOTHER man in your life right now (or EVER)?" she wrote in response to my blog post about a JDate fiasco. "You would probably wind up being a nurse for him. You should be a caregiver for YOURSELF."

Was my friend trying to guard me from a future I wouldn't allow myself to consider? Why indeed had I—now happily independent in my new downtown digs—signed up for JDate in the first place?

And why had I been spying on physically fit, gray-haired men at my health club?

Furthermore, why had I asked my paired-up friends to keep me in mind if they knew an older single male who met my criteria—e.g., strolled without the aid of a walker and drove at night?

"Someone to hug," I shot back, believing my pathetic answer would win sympathy and stall further scathing. My response seemed reasonable, but the more I thought about it, the more I realized it wasn't bodily contact I missed. After all, any number of friends and relatives would welcome my arms wrapped around their torso.

If not an embrace, what, then, had I been seeking in my attempts to find a date? To spot clues, I stretched out on the couch, closed my eyes, and reviewed past examples of familiar marriages. And what I came up with is this: I miss the feeling of being *adored*.

In my stroll through wedlock history, I realized Tommy spoiled me for future relationships. His frequent heartfelt emotions were a revelation because they were, unfortunately, missing from my first marriage and tragically one-sided in my parents'.

In my initial go-round, my husband and I appreciated, admired, and cared for each other. But did we *adore* each other? Perhaps in the stars-in-our-eyes early years, but after that, when our personal struggles blinded us, the word went missing.

My parents' marriage was so impressionable that it spurred my memoir, *The Division Street Princess*. As I wrote: Irv loved Min from the moment he saw the nineteen-year-old neighborhood beauty. But, alas, Min didn't return his ardor. It wasn't until her old-world mother urged, "You'll learn to love him" that Min accepted Irv's proposal.

Bubbie, you were wrong! Despite Dad's longing and his purchase of gifts he couldn't pay for—like the mink stole cradled in tissue and presented in a white box—Mom never grasped the lesson.

"Take it back; we can't afford it," I remember her saying as she stared at Dad's present. And bitty me, channeling my father's pining, pleaded, "Just try it on, Mom, just try it on." She did and, twirling in front of a full-length mirror like a 1940s movie star, decided to keep the mink while Dad paid for it in monthly installments.

I never did learn why Mom couldn't return Dad's adoration. I guess some of it could be linked to her disappointment in spending her pretty young life behind the counter of a grocery store on a tenement street. The neighborhood beauty deserved better.

So perhaps glum childhood scenes inspired me to take the part of my mother in my adult life. I would show her how an adored wife acts. When I found Tommy's love notes, I'd squeal as if they were hidden jewels. Then I'd get my own Post-it and draw a heart with the words "Love you, Hubber!" and tuck it into a gym shoe, a golf glove, or some other spot where he would later discover it.

Among the other mementos I saved was a letter Tommy wrote

to me early on. It was the one I read it to him as I sat on the other side of the metal railings of his hospice bed. It was two pages long, written in pen on yellow-lined paper, and began:

"My Darling Elaine, I don't know what lies ahead but I do know I want to spend the rest of my life loving you and taking care of you. We make a great team. When I think about all the years I was alone I realize now that you were the missing part of the puzzle that makes it all fit together."

That's what I'm talking about.

Acknowledgments

For help on everything from caring for and loving Tommy to reading and sharing my blogs to supporting my journey, I am grateful to the following people: Randy and Vicky Bates, Barry Bruner, Karen Carpino, Linda Chaput, Sara Clatanoff, Diane Cohen, Renee Elkin, Jennifer Estlin, Ruth Gilbert, Maureen Gorman, Alice Herman, Lisa Holton, Kingsbury Plaza staff, Jamison Linz, Marshall Lobin, Kristen Magee, Bonnie McGrath, Susan Messing, Hedy Ratner, Stuart Rivard, Lola Rivero, Ron and Jill Rohde, Milo Samardzija, Neil Shapiro, Norma Shapiro, Ron Shapiro, Faith Soloway, Jill Soloway, Harry Soloway, Tiger Temkin, and Holly and John Van Essen, and Susie Miller Tweedy.

For help on bringing this book to life, I am grateful to She Writes Press, particularly Brooke Warner, Cait Levin, Krissa Lagos, and Annie Tucker.

For creating my awesome Kickstarter video, I am grateful to Ben Hollis of Ben Hollis Worldwide, Inc. And for contributing to my Kickstarter campaign, I am beholden to the following people: Diane Cohen, Carol Niec, Teme and Jeff Ring, Jill Soloway, Linda Ruzan, Neal Pollack, Milan Samardzija, Lisa Holton, John Levenstein, Gary Rudoren, Adam Levy, Jenifer Strozier, Bill Linden, Nili Yelin Wronski, Tamara Ham, Chris Ruys, Carol Rosenthal, RP Ruzan, Kristen Magee, Sally Brooks, Julie Graber, Norman Levy, Johanna Stein, Carrie and Kevin Neustadt, Judy

Korin, Racelle Rosett, Susan Messing, Faith Soloway, Linda Benjamin, Jen Cohen, Tom Booker, Pam Victor, Ellen Stoneking, Annie Watson-Johnson, Jennifer Estlin, Suzanne Clores, Gail Flager, Steve Durning, Harry Soloway, Laura Diamond, Susan Miller Tweedy, Kathleen Naureckas, Peter Saltzman, Renee S. Elkin, Allison Vivian Fine, Susan Straus, Bonnie McGrath, Marcia Rosenthal, Delia O'Hara, Sheryl Rue-Borden, Ron Shapiro, Jan Kostner, Alison True, Gaven Carlton, Sheri Langendorf, Darylle Gilbert, Tracy Baim, Janet A. Keating, Bathsheba Nemerovski, Charles Otto, Rick O'Dell, Christine Bolt, Holly Vandenberg VanEssen, Sue Ontiveros, Tim and Penny Shultz, Rosalind Wattel, Ed and Ann Weisheimer, Roberta Wilk, Cheryl Blumenthal, Mary Grigar, Sara Clatanoff, Pepe Miller, Sara Miller Acosta, Jill W. Graham, Madeline Rabb, Alan Shapiro, Raiselle Resnick, Sarah Thyre, Marcia Elkin, Jen Braeden, Jen Lippman, Ben Zook, Candace Wayne, David Jacobson, Christine Kowalke, Devon Kirkpatrick, Ron Gould, Donald Segal, Michael Solarz, Paula Giroux, Dave Rodman, Hope Ross, Barb Halley, Beverly Sandock, Greg Lopatka, Della Leavitt, Cynthia Rogan, Susan Kraykowski, Hillary Carlip, Elizabeth Brandt, Jill Day, Randal Turner, Eric Waddell, Beth Urech, Berit Engen, Chris Altschuler, R. Janie Isackson, Sherri McGinnis Gonzales, Ruth Gilbert, Susan Marcus, Lynda Schiff, Vaso Georgulis Powers, Ian Harvie, Joseph J. Gabriel, Edwin B. Wald, Jackie Kaplan-Perkins, Karen Carpino, and Lawrence Green.

QUESTIONS FOR DISCUSSION

1. The title *Green Nails and Other Acts of Rebellion: Life After Loss* is taken from one of the book's chapters. Do you think it successfully encapsulates the point of the book? Or is there another you think would better interpret its contents?

2. In the book's title chapter, Elaine humorously rebels against some of her deceased husband's rigid views. How do you rebel in your own relationship?

3. *Green Nails* is divided between Elaine's caregiving journey and her transition into widowhood. Which part did you relate to more? Why?

4. In the very first chapter, "Now May I Shoot the Messenger?," Elaine is angry at the neurologist's callous pronouncement of Tommy's illness. Have you ever had a similar experience with the medical community?

5. Elaine writes about taking away her husband's keys when it becomes too dangerous for him to drive. This is a typical experience with older parents. Can you identify? Would you have handled it differently?

6. After reading this memoir, you probably have a sense of Tommy's character. How do you think he would feel about his exposure or treatment in the book?

7. Caregiving is a challenge for couples. Some rally; others break apart. Do you think Elaine's description of her compassionate behavior is realistic? Would more anger or resentment have been more believable?

8. Elaine believes that writing about her caregiving and widowhood experiences have been therapeutic for her. Have you ever used journaling, or other forms of writing, as therapy?

9. Before reading *Green Nails*, had you ever heard of frontotemporal degeneration or primary progressive aphasia? Does Elaine's story give you more insight into brain conditions?

10. Elaine's decision to bring Tommy home for hospice, rather than to a facility devoted to end-of-life care, causes controversy among her friends and family. Do you think her decision is wise? Does it serve Tommy well?

11. Elaine moves steadily along in her journey to widowhood. Do you believe her decision to sell her and Tommy's home and move on is made too quickly? Does she give herself enough time to grieve?

12. Towards the end of the book, Elaine writes about her dating experiences. After reading about her love for and devotion to Tommy, were these essays uplifting or jarring for you?

Resources

American Speech-Language-Hearing Association (www.asha. org) is the national professional, scientific, and credentialing association for more than 166,000 audiologists; speech-language pathologists; speech, language, and hearing scientists; audiology and speech-language pathology support personnel; and students.

Association for Frontotemporal Degeneration (www.theaftd. org) is the place for accurate information, compassion, and hope when lives are touched by frontotemporal degeneration (FTD), also called frontotemporal dementia or frontotemporal lobar degeneration (FTLD). The disease process causes a group of brain disorders characterized by changes in behavior and personality, language and/or motor skills, and a deterioration in a person's ability to function.

Elderwerks (www.elderwerks.com) is a free senior-housing and care-resource network for seniors, their families, and the professionals who help older adults. The company helps seniors through the transition from one home to another or with finding needed services.

Family Caregiver Alliance (www.caregiver.org) is a public voice for caregivers whose programs—information, education, services, research, and advocacy—support and sustain the work of families nationwide caring for loved ones with chronic, disabling health conditions.

Horizon Hospice & Palliative Care (www.horizonhospice.org) is a not-for-profit, community-based organization whose mission is to provide comfort for the dying, to preserve dignity at the end of life, and to educate the community.

Marbles: The Brain Store (www.marblesthebrainstore.com) is a retail store with a collection of handpicked, expert-tested, fun ways for all ages to develop a healthier brain.

Universal Medical ID (www.identifyyourself.com) offers medical IDs that, in a medical emergency, alert medics or other medical professionals to give prompt, precise treatment.

National Aphasia Association (www.aphasia.org) is a nonprofit organization that promotes public education, research, rehabilitation, and support services to assist people with aphasia and their families.

Northwestern University Feinberg School of Medicine (www. brain.northwestern.edu/dementia/ppa/index.html) houses the Cognitive Neurology and Alzheimer's Disease Center (CNADC), a multidepartmental, freestanding component of the Feinberg School of Medicine specializing in the clinical care and scientific study of neurological diseases that interfere with cognition and behavior. Areas of clinical emphasis include age-related memory impairments, dementia, Alzheimer's disease, frontotemporal degeneration, primary progressive aphasia, and related neurodegenerative conditions.

Senior Women Web (www.seniorwomen.com) is "an uncommon site for uncommon women" that attempts to reflect women's issues and concerns and the relationships of community and connectivity.

Widows List (www.widowslist.com) aims to provide a platform where women "in the widow 'hood" have a voice and can discuss their unique challenges, conflicts, solutions, and joys, families, friends, jobs, and leisure time.

About the Author

© Ron Gould, Ron Gould Studios

Elaine Soloway is the author of the memoir *The Division Street Princess*, the novel *She's Not The Type*, and a contributor to the anthology *Ask Me About My Divorce*. A public relations consultant for thirty years, she also writes the blogs *The Rookie Widow*, *The Rookie Caregiver*, and *Too Old To Talk Tech*. Along with developing her own essays, she is a writing coach and a tech tutor. Before launching her consulting business, she was a press aide to Chicago Mayor Jane Byrne and communications director for School Superintendent Ruth Love. Soloway is a lifelong Chicagoan and currently lives in the city's River North neighborhood.

SELECTED TITLES FROM SHE WRITES PRESS

She Writes Press is an independent publishing company
founded to serve women writers everywhere.
Visit us at www.shewritespress.com.

Splitting the Difference: A Heart-Shaped Memoir by Tré Miller-Rodríguez
$19.95, 978-1-938314-20-9
When 34-year-old Tré Miller-Rodríguez's husband dies suddenly from
a heart attack, her grief sends her on an unexpected journey that cul-
minates in a reunion with the biological daughter she gave up at 18.

Where Have I Been All My Life? A Journey Toward Love and Wholeness
by Cheryl Rice $16.95, 978-1-63152-917-7
Rice's universally relatable story of how her mother's sudden death
launched her on a journey into the deepest parts of grief—and, ulti-
mately, toward love and wholeness.

Her Beautiful Brain: A Memoir by Ann Hedreen
$16.95, 978-1-938314-92-6
The heartbreaking story of a daughter's experiences as her beautiful,
brainy mother begins to lose her mind to an unforgiving disease:
Alzheimer's.

Breathe: A Memoir of Motherhood, Grief, and Family Conflict
by Kelly Kittel $16.95, 978-1-938314-78-0
A mother's heartbreaking account of losing two sons in the span of
nine months—and learning, despite all the obstacles in her way, to find
joy in life again.

A Leg to Stand On: An Amputee's Walk into Motherhood
by Colleen Haggerty $16.95, 978-1-63152-923-8
Haggerty's candid story of how she overcame the pain of losing a leg at
seventeen—and of terminating two pregnancies as a young woman—
and went on to become a mother, despite her fears.

Four Funerals and a Wedding: Resilience in a Time of Grief
by Jill Smolowe $16.95, 978-1-938314-72-8
When journalist Jill Smolowe lost four family members in less than two
years, she turned to modern bereavement research for answers—and
made some surprising discoveries.

10/15 ① 1/15
5/17 ⑧ 3/17

CPSIA information can be obtained at www.ICGtesting.com
Printed in the USA
LVOW12s2159121114